PRENTICE HALL MATHEMATICS

ALGEBRA 1
GEOMETRY
ALGEBRA 2

Technology Activities

PEARSON

Prentice
Hall

Needham, Massachusetts
Upper Saddle River, New Jersey

ISBN: 0-13-063380-1

5 6 7 8 9 10   06 05 04

Technology Activities

Contents

Introduction

This technology handbook contains a wide variety of activities designed to supplement your high school mathematics curriculum. Specifically, these activities are correlated to Prentice Hall's *Algebra 1*, *Algebra 2*, and *Geometry* texts. While each of these books contains a wide variety of technology-related activities, the activities contained in this handbook provide a means to extend many mathematical ideas through a medium that is both practical and engaging. In particular, you will find that these activities use technology in a way that allows students to explore ideas in a way that is often unobtainable by traditional methods.

The CBL 2™ (Calculator-Based Laboratory 2) activities can be used with both *Algebra 1* and *Algebra 2*. The CBL 2 offers an excellent opportunity to collect real-world data that can be analyzed by a TI-83/TI-83 Plus graphing calculator. Each of these activities addresses a specific skill(s), which can be correlated to different sections of your text. Refer to the correlation chart included in the table of contents for help choosing appropriate lessons for each activity. The CBL 2 activities can be adapted as a whole class demonstration or small groups, depending on the availability of resources.

The *Algebra 1* and *Algebra 2* activities make exclusive use of the TI-83/TI-83 Plus graphing calculator. These activities follow an "Investigate" and "Exercises" format, which can be completed in a small group setting with limited teacher support. Students are guided through a series of steps where they learn how to use the technology to explore the specific ideas being addressed. The exercises that follow each investigation offer students an opportunity to further enhance their understanding of the material. Some of these activities include an extension that can be assigned at the discretion of the teacher.

The *Geometry* section of the handbook has been designed around the *Geometer's Sketchpad* software package. Constructions made with this dynamic geometry software are made in such a way that they reinforce the ideas presented in the text. For example, regular polygons are constructed by using an angle of rotation equal to the measure of one interior angle. As another example, parallel lines are made by first selecting a line and a point not on the line. This supports *Euclid's Parallel Postulate,* which states that "through a point not on a line, there is one and only one line parallel to the given line."

The geometry activities follow a "Construct," "Investigate," and "Extend" format. As with the *Algebra* activities, these activities can be completed in small groups (or individually) as computer availability permits.

Finally, the web-based activities are related to all three texts. Four of these activities are correlated to *Algebra 1* and *Algebra 2*. The remaining two activities can be used with *Geometry*. These activities provide students with a better understanding as to how the Internet can be a valuable research tool. It is important to verify that students have been permitted access to the Internet *and* that the policies of your particular school district are not compromised. The instructor may want to set guidelines as to how to search for information and credit the sources used.

As a general rule, these activities assume a working knowledge of the technologies being used. For more information on the TI-83/TI-83 Plus graphing calculators, consult your guidebook or go to http://www.phschool.com (and click on the link for TI-83/83 Plus procedures). Information on how to use the CBL 2 can be found in the manufacturer's guidebook or at http://education.ti.com. Consult the Geometer's Sketchpad user's guide for more information on how to use Geometer's Sketchpad.

General Information for CBL 2

CBL 2™ activities are designed to provide students with a method to explore real-world applications of algebra. These activities can be used at any algebra level and with any textbook. They are intended specifically to support *Algebra 1* and *Algebra 2*.

You can use these activities in at least three different ways:

- *To introduce a chapter or lesson*
  Use an activity to introduce new ideas and connections or as an interactive example for a new topic.

- *To close a chapter or lesson*
  Use an activity for a final project or to assess students' understanding.

- *During a chapter or lesson*
  Use an activity as an exercise or for classroom discussion.

The CBL 2 activities located in this handbook can be used as whole-class experiments (by using the TI View Screen) or small group (by linking the data to students' calculators).

CBL 2 activities can motivate and challenge students to learn more about math and science. They provide ample opportunity to incorporate algebra into real-world situations.

EQUIPMENT

The following special hardware is necessary for the activities in this booklet.

> TI CBL 2 unit (kit includes 3 probes: temperature probe, voltage probe, and light probe)
> Vernier Ultrasonic Motion Detector
> graphing calculator compatible with the CBL 2 unit
> unit-to-unit link cable
> TI View Screen (recommended)
> TI Graph Link with computer access (recommended)

PROGRAMS

The CBL 2 is equipped with a built-in program called DataMate which can be transferred to the TI-83/TI-83 Plus with the unit-to-unit link cable. The DataMate program is initially loaded by using **2nd** [LINK] and select **RECEIVE** from the TI-83/TI-83 Plus. Use the TRANSFER button on the CBL 2 to send the program. All CBL 2 activities located in this handbook can be run using DataMate although other programs, such as those used with the original CBL™ systems, also run on the CBL 2. On the TI-83 Plus, DataMate is run from the APPS menu; for other calculators, it is run from the calculator's program menu. Software programs for the CBL 2 can be downloaded from http://www.vernier.com/calc/index.html. The TI Graph Link software and cable are necessary to transfer software from a computer to the CBL 2 unit.

BASIC STEPS

The basic steps that are followed when conducting an experiment with the CBL 2™ are as follows:

1. Connect a sensor(s) to the CBL 2 unit, connect the CBL 2 to a calculator, and run the DataMate or CBL 2 compatible program.

2. Collect the data.

3. Graph the data.

4. Analyze the data.

The CBL 2 is capable of automatically detecting most sensors that are connected to the unit. After the sensor is detected, the CBL 2 loads a default "Time Graph" experiment that collects data at a pre-determined rate. These settings can be manually adjusted if necessary.

USING THE DATAMATE APPLICATION

After the DataMate program is started, a main menu screen appears. An auto-ID sensor will be automatically detected by the CBL 2 as seen in the screen at right. Use the **SETUP** command (see next section) if the sensor is not auto-ID.

```
CH 1: TEMP(C)        24.5



MODE: TIME GRAPH-180

1:SETUP      4:ANALYZE
2:START      5:TOOLS
3:GRAPH      6:QUIT
```

Analog Sensors (CH 1, CH 2, CH 3)

Select **2 : START** to begin the data collection. After data has been collected, the graph is automatically displayed and re-scaled (if there are 2 or more sensors attached to the unit, you are prompted to select a channel to graph from the graph menu). Press ENTER to return to the main screen.

Motion Detector (DIG/SONIC)

After collecting data, you will be prompted to select 'DISTANCE', 'VELOCITY', or 'ACCELERATION'. With the arrow positioned to the left of 'DIG-DISTANCE', press ENTER to see the graph of time verses distance.

SETTING UP AN ANALOG CHANNEL (CH 1, CH 2, CH 3)

To select or remove a sensor from one of the analog channels, press **1 : SETUP** from the main screen. Use the up/down arrow keys to position the arrow to the left of the appropriate channel and press ENTER . Select a channel from the list or press **7 : MORE** for more options. To clear the channel, continue to press **7 : MORE** until '2: NONE' appears. Choose this option to clear the channel.

SETTING UP THE DIG/SONIC CHANNEL

To select or clear the motion detector, press **1 : SETUP** from the main screen. Use the up/down arrow keys to position the arrow to the left of the DIG channel and press ENTER . Select **1 : MOTION(M)** for meters, **2 : MOTION(FT)** for feet, or **3 : NONE** to clear the channel.

CHANGING TIME GRAPH SETTINGS

For each sensor, DataMate loads a default time graph experiment. In this booklet, the sensors used have the following default time graph settings:

	Y-Min	Y-Max	Sample Interval	No. of Samples
Motion Detector (M)	0	6	0.05	100
Motion Detector (Ft.)	1	20	0.05	100
Temperature Probe (C)	–20	125	1	180
Temperature Probe (F)	–5	260	1	180
Voltage Probe (V)	–10	10	0.1	180

To change the time graph settings, press **1 : SETUP** from the DataMate Main Screen. Press the up and down arrows to move the cursor to MODE and press ENTER . Choose **2 : TIME GRAPH** to see the current settings. To change the time graph settings press **2 : CHANGE TIME SETTINGS.** Enter the TIME BETWEEN SAMPLES IN SECONDS and the NUMBER OF SAMPLES. The EXPERIMENT LENGTH will be automatically calculated after pressing ENTER .

Note As a general rule:

- Collect 180 data points or less when using 1 sensor

- Collect 90 data points or less when using 2 sensors

- Collect 60 data points or less when using 3 sensors

Note Use the rule "Experiment Length = Time Interval × Number of Samples" to determine the value of each parameter.

SELECTING SUBSETS OF DATA

Sometimes, students need only a subset of a data set. For example, when a book is dropped, the only interesting data is for the falling book, not the book at rest. The excess data should be removed before any models are applied.

To remove excess data, select **2 : SELECT REGION** from the Graph Menu Screen. Use the arrow keys to position the cursor at a point that marks the left boundary of the desired region and press ENTER . Repeat this process to select the right boundary. You will be prompted to wait a few moments before seeing the re-scaled graph.

ANALYZING DATA

From the DataMate main screen, select **4 : ANALYZE.** Option **2 : CURVE FIT** allows you to select that regression type that best matches the data. After selecting the appropriate regression model, the calculator automatically determines the equation of best fit. Press ENTER to see the curve graphed along with the data points.

```
      CURVEFIT
1:LINEAR(CH1 VS TIME)
2:LINEAR(CH2 VS TIME)
3:LINEAR(CH3 VS TIME)
4:LINEAR(DIST VS TIME)
5:LINEAR(VELO VS TIME)
6:LINEAR(CH2 VS CH1)
7:MORE
```

LOCATING WHERE THE DATA IS STORED

When data is collected from a single sensor, it is stored according to the table below.

Data Type	Time	CH1	CH2	CH3	Distance (D)	Velocity (V)	Acceleration (A)
Where Stored	L1	L2	L3	L4	L6	L7	L8

LINKING TWO CALCULATORS

The data collected by the CBL 2 unit is stored only in the calculator connected to the CBL 2 unit. Ideally, every calculator in the classroom should have the completed data.

Two TI-83/TI-83 Plus Calculators

- Link the calculators with the link cable. Push the link cable all the way into the calculators. Turn on both calculators.

- On the receiving calculator, press **2nd** [LINK] and select **RECEIVE**

- On the sending calculator, press **2nd** [LINK] **4.** Move the arrow to a list you wish to transfer and press **ENTER** . This changes the arrow into a square. Repeat for every list you wish to transfer. Press ▶ **ENTER** to transmit the data. The word DONE appears when every list has been sent.

SELECTING POINTS

Throughout the activities students are asked to select points from a plot of data or from a graph of a model. For example, two methods are demonstrated below for finding the vertex of a parabola. These methods can be used after you have quit the DataMate program and graphed the appropriate list(s) and/or regression equation(s).

When working with lists:

Use **TRACE** if the vertex appears to be an actual data point. Press **TRACE** and use the arrow keys to move the cursor to the point that best represents the vertex. The coordinates of the selected point appear at the bottom of the screen.

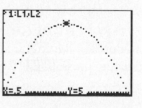

If the vertex does not appear to be an actual point, use vertical and horizontal lines from the DRAW menu. From the graph, press **2nd** [DRAW] **4** and use the arrow keys to move the line to the best location. The *x*-coordinate appears at the bottom of the screen. Use a horizontal line (press **2nd** [DRAW] **3**) to find the *y*-coordinate of the vertex (the vertical line will disappear, however, a blinking cursor will be located on the horizontal line where the vertical line would have passed).

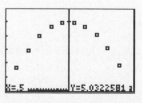

When working with regression equations:

Use **2nd** [CALC] to evaluate the regression equation for specified values; locate zeros; find maximum and minimum values, and locate a point of intersection of two graphs.

OTHER NOTES

- These activities assume that only one set of equipment is available and that the entire class performs each activity. If multiple sets of equipment are available, the activities can be done in smaller groups. In that case, the calculators should be linked only within each group.

- It is helpful to use the overhead view screen when conducting experiments for an entire class.

- When finding a specific point from the plot, such as an *x*-intercept, it is more accurate to find a model of the data and then find the specific point from the model.

CBL 2 UNIT TIPS

- The CBL 2™ unit can use a probe to measure data without connecting it to a calculator. After attaching an auto-ID probe, press **QUICK SETUP.** The unit will automatically scan for the attached sensor(s); when the yellow light flashes, the unit is ready to collect data. Press the **START/STOP** button to collect the data (the green light flashes as the data is being collected). The data is stored in the CBL 2 memory and can be transferred using the DataMate program at a later time.

- The DATADIR program (available for download at www.ti.com/calc) can be used to store programs in the CBL 2's *FLASH* memory. This is particularly useful if you want to run programs that are already stored on your calculator but need to be stored elsewhere.

- The temperature probe, voltage probe, and light probe must be connected to one of the three analog channels (CH1, CH2, CH3). Always connect sensors to the channels in numerical order. The Ultrasonic Motion Detector should be plugged into the other channel (DIG/SONIC).

- For more information, refer to *Getting Started with CBL 2*, available from Texas Instruments.

VERNIER ULTRASONIC MOTION DETECTOR

- The motion detector measures distance by emitting an ultrasonic signal. It then measures the time the signal takes to reflect off an object and return to the detector.

- The motion detector works best if it is measuring the distance to a smooth, flat object. For this reason, do not use a fuzzy ball, such as a tennis ball. The motion detector also works well with people.

- The motion detector works best if the object is no closer than 1.5 feet (about 0.5 m) and no farther than 20 feet (about 6 m).

- When using the motion detector, make sure that it remains motionless and that nothing interferes with the path of its signal. Keep the CBL 2 unit's cords away from the front of the motion detector. Students should not move into the path of the signal during measuring.

- For more information, refer to the user's pages that come with the motion detector.

Take a Walk, Part 1

Activity 1

Set-up

Create a clear pathway in the classroom. Place a motion detector on a table facing this pathway. The motion detector measures the distance to an object. In this case, the object is a student walking in front of the motion detector. The student must be directly in front of the motion detector, but no closer than 1.5 ft. Run the program DATAMATE and select **2 : START** from the main screen each time a student walks.

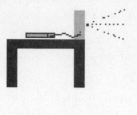

WHAT YOU'LL LEARN
- Plotting and interpreting points on an axis

- Finding rate of change from graphs

- Relating slope to rate of change

WHAT YOU'LL NEED
CBL 2™ unit, graphing calculator compatible with CBL 2, motion detector

Time Graph Settings (Mode: Time Graph–7.2)

- Time Interval = 0.06

- Number of Samples = 120

Channel Settings

- DIG: MOTION (FT)

Pre-Activity Questions

1. The motion detector records the distance to an object. The graphing calculator plots this distance with respect to time. Each point in the plot at the right represents a reading of distance versus time. How far is each object from the detector? How long after the program started was each measurement taken?

   a. point *A*   **b.** point *B*

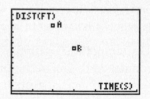

2. Draw a point that represents the measurement of an object 10 ft from the detector that is recorded 4 s after the program starts.

3. How should you walk so that the plot from this point to a new point will be a line with positive slope?

Activity

Run the program DATAMATE and press **2 : START.** After the second set of two beeps, have a student walk so that the plot appears as a line with positive slope.

4. Sketch the plot from the calculator on a graph like the one at the right. Link the data (located in **L1** and **L6**) to the other students in the class.

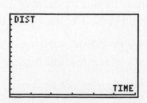

5. How can you find how fast the student walked? In what units is the speed measured?

6. Use the arrow keys to trace along the graph and find the starting distance and the beginning time. Then find the final distance and the ending time. Use these two points to determine the average speed of the student.

Take a Walk, Part 1 (continued)

7. Speed is the rate of change in location over time. How does speed relate to the slope of a line? Define slope.

8. Predict the plot for a student walking faster than the first student.

9. On the graph like the one at the right, sketch the line for a student who walked faster than the student whose line is shown.

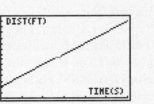

10. Using the same graph, sketch the line of a slower student.

11. Perform the activity again but have the student walk faster than the first student's speed. Find the average speed of the student.

12. Perform the activity again but have the student walk slower than the first student's speed. Find the average speed of the student.

13. How would someone walk so that the plot is slanted downward from left to right?

14. How would someone walk so that the plot was a horizontal line? A vertical line?

15. The *y*-intercept is the point where a line intersects the *y*-axis. In each plot drawn by the graphing calculator, what does the *y*-intercept represent?

16. Describe the motion of the walker recorded on each graph.

a. 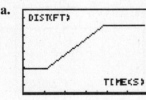   b. 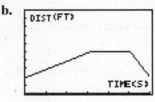   c.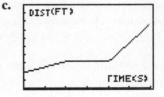

17. In Exercise 16b, did the walker start and end at the same location? Explain.

18. In Exercise 16b, did the walker walk faster moving away from the motion detector or moving toward it? Explain.

Take a Walk, Part 2

Activity 2

Set-up

Create a clear pathway in the classroom. Place a motion detector on a table facing this pathway. The motion detector measures the distance to an object. In this case, the object is a student walking in front of the motion detector. The student must be directly in front of the motion detector, but no closer than 1.5 ft. Have another student run the program DATAMATE by selecting **2 : START** from the main screen each time a student walks.

Time Graph Settings (Mode: Time Graph–7.2)

- Time Interval = 0.06

- Number of Samples = 120

Channel Settings

- DIG: MOTION (FT)

Pre-Activity Questions

1. Suppose points *A* and *B* are two data points taken by the CBL 2™ unit from a student's walk. What is the sign of the slope of the line connecting *A* and *B*? What is the sign of the *y*-intercept?

2. On a graph like the one shown at right, draw a line through *A* starting at the origin. Draw a line through *B* starting at the origin. Which line has the steeper slope? What is the slope of that line?

3. Is the line that passes through *A* a direct variation? If so, write the equation of the line.

What You'll Learn
- Intercepting slopes and *y*-intercepts in a real-world setting

- Finding the slope of a line

- Writing the equation of a line in slope-intercept form

What You'll Need
CBL 2™ unit, graphing calculator compatible with CBL 2, motion detector, watch with a second hand

Activity

Run the program DATAMATE and press **2 : START.** After the second set of two beeps, have a student walk so that the plot appears as a line with positive slope.

4. Sketch the plot from the calculator on a graph like the one at the right. Link all the calculators in class so each student has the same data. The *x*-values are in **L1** and the *y*-values are in **L6**.

5. Find the *y*-intercept of the graph. What is the significance of the *y*-intercept?

6. Create a scatter plot of the data and use TRACE to pick two points from the plot and find their coordinates. Be careful not to choose points that lie off the line of the graph.

7. Find the slope of the line containing the points you chose in Exercise 6.

Take a Walk, Part 2 (continued)

· ·

8. One form of a linear equation is the slope-intercept form, which is written $y = mx + b$ where m is the slope and b is the y-intercept. Write the equation of the line from the graph in slope-intercept form.

9. Use a graphing calculator to graph the equation you found in Exercise 8 on the same screen as the data points. How well does your equation model the data? Explain.

10. Compare your model to those of other students in the class. Which model do you feel is best? Why?

11. For what values of x will your model predict reasonable y-values? Explain.

12. Run DATAMATE again and perform a linear regression on the data. How well does your model compare with the model found by the calculator?

Perform the activity again. This time, the student who is walking should stand still for 2 s and then begin walking away from the motion detector at a constant speed. Have a student use a watch with a second hand to time the two seconds. This student should dictate when to begin the program and when the student should begin walking.

13. Sketch the plot from the calculator. Link all the calculators in class so each student has the same data. The x-values are in **L1** and the y-values are in **L6**.

14. Find a linear equation to model the student's walk. Compare your equation with the regression equation determined by the calculator.

15. Does the y-intercept have any significance? Explain.

16. Does the slope have any significance? Explain.

Synchronized Strut

Activity 3

Set-up

Two students walk and another student measures distances. Clear a wide pathway in the classroom for two people to walk with room between them. Place the two motion detectors far enough apart that the students are not too close. The students walk away from the detectors in the same direction. Have a student mark the starting and ending points of each walk with masking tape. Run the program DATAMATE each time the student walks.

Time Graph Settings (Mode: Time Graph–7.2)

- Time Interval = 0.06

- Number of Samples = 120

Channel Settings

- DIG: MOTION (FT)

Pre-Activity Questions

1. Predict the shapes of graphs that represent two students starting from the same place and walking at different speeds. Sketch them on the graph like the one at the right.

   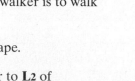

2. Sketch your prediction of a graph of two students starting at different places but walking at the same speed.

3. Sketch your prediction of a graph of two students starting at the same place and walking at the same speed.

What You'll Learn
- Finding slope and *y*-intercepts of a line

- Writing linear equations in slope-intercept form

- Comparing graphs of distance with respect to time

What You'll Need
Two CBL 2™ units, two graphing calculators compatible with CBL 2, two motion detectors, masking tape, measuring tape

Activity

Have each walker stand 1.5 ft away from a motion detector. One walker is to walk faster than the other. Run the DATAMATE program.

4. Measure the distance each student walks with a measuring tape.

5. Link the two calculators and transmit **L6** from one calculator to **L2** of the other calculator. Using the calculator with all three lists, turn on **Plot1** for **L1** and **L2** and **Plot2** for **L1** and **L6**. Use **ZoomStat** to view both graphs. Sketch the graphs. How do they compare to your prediction in Exercise 1?

The graphs should look similar to the sample at right. If so, link the data to the other students in the class.

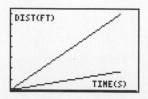

6. Which point is on both graphs from Exercise 5? Why?

7. Use **TRACE** to determine the *y*-intercept of both graphs.

8. Find the slope of each line.

Synchronized Strut (continued)

9. Write the equations in slope-intercept form of the two lines that represent the two walkers.

10. What do the slopes represent?

11. Why is the slope different for each graph?

12. To confirm that the slopes differ, use TRACE to find the distance of each walker at 2 s. The *x*-value is time and the *y*-value is distance.

13. Who walked farther in 2 s?

Repeat the activity, but this time have one student start 1 ft farther from the motion detector. Ask students to walk at about the same speed.

14. Measure the distance each student walks with a measuring tape.

15. Link the two calculators and transmit **L6** from one calculator to **L2** of the other calculator. Using the calculator with all three lists, turn on **Plot1** for **L1** and **L2** and **Plot2** for **L1** and **L6**. Use ZOOM **9 : ZoomStat** to view both graphs. Sketch the graphs.

The graphs should look similar to the sample at right. If so, link the data to the other students in the class.

16. Calculate the slope of each line. What do you find?

17. What can you conclude about any lines that appear parallel?

18. Which variable in the $y = mx + b$ form of the equation of a line is similar for both graphs?

19. Find the equation of each line. Use this algebraic model to predict the position of each walker at 15 s by substituting 15 for *x*. Then use the model to predict the position at 20 s. What is the difference in the positions of the walkers at each time? What does this tell you about their speeds?

20. Without running the experiment again, what can you predict about the graphs of the equations of two walkers who start from the same place and walk the same speed?

Coming and Going

Activity 4

Set-up

Clear a wide pathway in the classroom so that two students can walk freely. Turn a table perpendicular to the pathway as shown in the diagram. Place the motion detectors on opposite ends of the table facing toward the cleared pathway. With a stopwatch, one student measures the time from when the walkers start until they pass each other. A second student uses a yardstick to measure the distance from the table to the passing point. One walker stands about 20 ft away from one motion detector and walks slowly toward the table. The other walker starts about 1.5 ft from the second motion detector and walks slowly away from the table.

Finally, two students should operate the two graphing calculators.

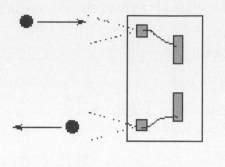

What You'll Learn
- Interpreting the intersection of two lines in a real-world setting

- Finding the intersection of two lines

- Solving a system of equations by graphing

What You'll Need
Two CBL 2™ units, two graphing calculators compatible with CBL 2, two motion detectors

Time Graph Settings (Mode: Time Graph–6)

- Time Interval = 0.06

- Number of Samples = 120

Channel Settings

- DIG: MOTION (FT)

Pre-Activity Questions

1. Can one motion detector detect two students simultaneously? Relate your answer to functions.

2. Suppose two motion detectors measure data simultaneously. One detector measures a student walking toward it. The second detector measures a student walking away from it. Sketch a graph representing both sets of data on a graph like the one at the right. Explain the significance of the y-intercepts and slopes.

3. Would the point where the two walkers pass each other be measured by the motion detectors?

Activity

Run the program DATAMATE on each calculator. Have the marker indicate when everyone should begin. The two graphing calculator operators should press **2 : START** at the same time. After the second set of two beeps, the students begin walking and the timer starts the stopwatch. When the two students pass, the timer stops the stopwatch and records the time when they met. The marker marks the position on the floor and measures the distance from the table.

Coming and Going (continued)

Link the two calculators and transmit **L6** from one calculator to **L2** of the other calculator. Using the calculator with all three lists, turn on **Plot1** for **L1** and **L2** and **Plot2** for **L1** and **L6**. Use [ZOOM] **9 : ZoomStat** to view both graphs. If your data looks like the sample at right, link the data to the other calculators. Be sure to transmit **L1, L2,** and **L6.**

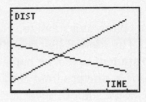

4. Turn on **Plot1** for **L1** and **L2** and **Plot2** for **L1** and **L6.** Use [TRACE] to find the *y*-intercept of each data line. Press ▼ ▲ to move to the other plot. Round your answers to two decimal places.

5. Use [TRACE] to find two other points on each line. Do not choose points that lie off of the main data lines.

6. Use your points found in Exercise 5 to find the slope of each line. Round your answers to two decimal places.

7. Write a linear equation to model the data for each walker.

8. Enter the equations as **Y1** and **Y2.** Press [GRAPH] to see the models and the data. How well do the lines model the data for the two walkers? If a line is not a good model, repeat Exercises 4–7 to find a better model.

9. The two models allow you to predict the location of each walker at any time. Solve the system of linear equations formed by the two models to determine where and when the walkers met. Round your answers to two decimal places.

10. Use the [2nd] [CALC] **5 : intersect** option of the calculator. Make sure you choose the two models, **Y1** and **Y2,** not the plots. What is the point of intersection of the two models? Check that your answer agrees with your answer from Exercise 9.

11. The actual location of the meeting was measured by the marker and the timer. Compare their measurements with your calculations from Exercises 9 and 10. Explain any discrepancies.

12. Explain why the two motion detectors were needed. Relate your answer to the definition of a function.

13. Perform the activity again. This time have one student remain still to produce a horizontal line. The other student walks past him or her in either direction. Find the models for each walker. Find the point of intersection.

Keep Your Eye on the Ball

Activity 5

Set-up

Use the clamp and stand to set up the motion detector about 5 ft above the ground. The motion detector should be parallel to and facing the ground. A second student holds the ball about 1.5 ft below the motion detector. A third student runs the program DATAMATE on the calculator. Be sure that the ball bounces on a smooth, level surface.

Time Graph Settings (Mode: Time Graph–4)

- Time Interval = 0.04

- Number of Samples = 100

Channel Settings

- DIG: MOTION (FT)

Pre-Activity Questions

1. When a ball bounces it rebounds to a maximum height that is less than the maximum height of the previous bounce. On a graph like the one shown at right, sketch a graph of a bouncing ball whose height changes over time.

2. Will the time that elapses between each bounce increase, decrease, or remain the same?

3. Is there a relationship between the maximum height of one bounce and the maximum height of the following rebound? Explain.

> **What You'll Learn**
> - Graphing a quadratic equation
>
> - Using a quadratic model to represent real-world data
>
> **What You'll Need**
> CBL 2™ unit, graphing calculator compatible with CBL 2, motion detector, a racquetball or other non-fuzzy ball, clamp with stand

Activity

The student running the program DATAMATE presses **2 : START.** The second set of two beeps signals the other student to drop the ball and move away quickly so that the motion of the student's hand is not picked up by the motion detector. Make sure that the ball bounces straight up and down and that the motion detector is held steady. When you are satisfied with the data, exit the DATAMATE program.

Enter the command 'max(L6) − L6 → L6' on the home screen. This will invert the data that represents height. Graph the data in an appropriate viewing window and verify that it resembles the screen at right. If it does, link **L1** and **L6** to the other members of the class.

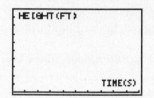

4. Use TRACE to find the maximum height of each bounce.

5. Find the differences in the maximum heights.

6. Is the change in the maximum heights a constant, or does it vary?

7. If it varies, are the differences increasing or decreasing?

8. Some advertisements claim a racquetball rebounds from 75% to 80% of the maximum height of the previous bounce. How can you check this claim?

Keep Your Eye on the Ball (continued)

9. Find the rebound percentages between each pair of consecutive bounces. Do you find a pattern? If so, what is it?

10. Each bounce is approximately the shape of a parabola. Each bounce can be approximated by a quadratic equation in standard form $y = ax^2 + bx + c$, where x represents time and y represents height. Find the point of maximum height for the first complete bounce. This point will be the vertex of the model parabola. Round the coordinates of the point to two decimal places.

11. Recall that the x-coordinate of the vertex of a parabola equals $-\dfrac{b}{2a}$. Solve this equation for b. Then substitute the x-value from Exercise 10 to find an equation for b in terms of a.

12. Substitute the value of b that you found in Exercise 11 into the standard form of a quadratic equation.

13. Substitute for x and y, using the coordinates of the vertex you found in Exercise 11, and solve the equation for c in terms of a. Substitute this value of c into the equation from Exercise 12.

14. Use TRACE to find the coordinates of one of the x-intercepts (or lowest points on the bounce) of the first complete bounce. Substitute these values for x and y into the equation from Exercise 13 and solve for a.

15. Now, use the value of a to write the equation of the model parabola. Round your values of a, b, and c to two decimal places.

16. Compare your model to the real data by graphing them on the same screen as the bounces on the graphing calculator.

Race Cars

Activity 6

Set-up

Place a motion detector on top of a couple of books facing into an open path into the room. You are going to run toy cars away from the motion detector. There will be at least two different types of toy cars. One car will be battery powered. The other should be a spring-loaded or wind-up car.

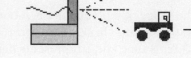

Time Graph Settings (Mode: Time Graph–1.6)

- Time Interval = 0.02

- Number of Samples = 80

Channel Settings

- DIG: MOTION (FT)

Pre-Activity Questions

1. The motion detector records distance with respect to time. Each car drives away from the motion detector. Will the graphs appear different? Explain.

2. Drive the cars along the floor without running the CBL 2 unit. On a graph like the one at right, sketch what the motion detector will record for each car. Label each graph.

3. What type of function will best model the data the motion detector records? Explain.

> **What You'll Learn**
> - Finding a real-world significance for slope
>
> - Writing a linear equation to model data
>
> - Using a model to make predictions
>
> **What You'll Need**
> CBL 2™ unit, graphing calculator compatible with CBL 2, motion detector, battery powered car, wind-up toy car

```
DIST




                    TIME
```

Activity

Place the battery-powered car about 1.5 ft away from the motion detector, facing away from the detector. Have a student run the program DATAMATE. Press **2 : START** on the calculator and have another student start the car after the second set of two beeps. Link the data to the other students in the class.

4. Sketch the plot from the calculator. What type of function is the best model for the car's motion?

5. Using paper and pencil, find an equation to model the motion of the car. What is the significance of the slope and *y*-intercept?

6. Exit DATAMATE and graph your model on the graphing calculator along with the data collected with the CBL 2 unit. Does your equation model the data well?

7. Use TRACE to find the initial and final data points. Find the slope between these points. This is the average speed of the car during its trip.

Race Cars (continued)

· ·

8. Compare your answer from Exercise 7 with the slope of your model. Explain any difference.

9. What is a realistic domain of your model? Explain.

10. The program DATAMATE collects data for 1.6 s at a fast rate. What differences would you expect in the graph if you collected data over a span of 6 seconds?

Repeat the activity with the battery-powered car. This time use a time interval of 0.06 s and collect 100 samples. Be sure that your car starts from the same location. When you are finished, link the data located in **L1** and **L6** to the other students in the class.

11. Find an equation to model the new data for the car's motion. Compare your new model with your old model.

12. Use your second model to find the speed of the car. Do you get the same answer as before?

13. What is a reasonable domain for this model?

14. Assume that the batteries in the car will not run down. How far can the car go in 10 s? In 2 min?

Run the program DATAMATE with the original time graph settings. Wind up the spring-loaded car. Place the car on the floor, facing away from the motion detector, about 1.5 ft away. Press **2 : START** on the graphing calculator and release the car after the second set of two beeps.

15. Sketch the plot from the calculator. Is this graph what you expected from a wind-up car? Explain. Relate what you expected to see to the method that the car uses to get its power.

16. Re-run the experiment with the spring-loaded car but use a time interval of 0.06 s with 100 samples. Remember that this configuration extends the experiment length to 6 s. Discuss the graph that results. In your discussion compare the results from using the two configurations.

Back and Forth It Goes

Activity 7

Set-up

Place two tables less than 1 m apart in a clear area in your classroom. Stack books on each table so that the top of each stack is more than 1 m from the floor. Bridge the two stacks with a meter stick. Place additional books on the meter stick to hold it in place. Attach a piece of string to a non-fuzzy ball like a racquetball. Hang the string from the center of the meter stick. Set the motion detector on a stack of books so that the grill has the same height as the resting ball. The detector must be at least 0.5 m from the ball when the ball is pulled toward the detector at a 20° angle.

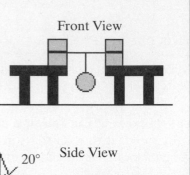
Front View

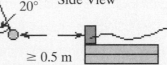
20° Side View

≥ 0.5 m

What You'll Learn
- Solving quadratic equations

- Using a model to make predictions

What You'll Need
CBL 2™ unit, graphing calculator compatible with CBL 2, motion detector, at least 2 m of string, racquetball or other non-fuzzy ball, meter stick, stopwatch, method to suspend pendulum

Time Graph Settings (Mode: Time Graph–5)

- Time Interval = 0.02

- Number of Samples = 100

Channel Settings

- DIG: MOTION (FT)

Pre-Activity Questions

1. The motion detector records the distance to the ball as it swings. Predict what the data will look like by sketching it on a graph like the one at right.

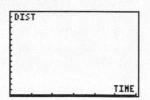

2. The period of a swing is the time it takes for one complete swing. If the length of the string is decreased will the period of the swing increase or decrease? If the length is increased?

Activity

Use a length of string of about 0.5 m. Set the motion detector at the same height as the ball at rest. Start the program DATAMATE. Pull the ball back at a 20° angle toward the motion detector. Have another student press **2 : START** while the student releases the ball after the second set of two beeps. When finished, link that data (located in **L1** and **L6**) to the other members of the class.

3. Sketch the graph displayed on the calculator attached to the motion detector. Is this what you expected?

4. Label the points where the ball is closest to and farthest from the detector. Does the motion detector record the actual nearest or farthest point? Explain.

Back and Forth It Goes (continued)

5. Use **TRACE** to find the x-coordinates of two adjacent maximums or minimums. You can also use the **2nd** [DRAW] feature (if DATAMATE is not running) to place a vertical line on the graph. The screen at right shows an example. Use ◄ and ► to move the line to the center of a peak or trough to find its x-coordinate.

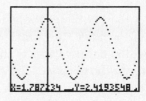

6. Find the difference between the two x-values you found in Exercise 5. This is the period of one complete swing.

7. Measure the length of the string precisely using the meter stick.

8. Enter your answers for the length and the period from Exercises 6–7 into **L3** and **L4** on a graphing calculator. Let **L3** be the period and **L4** be the length of the string.

9. Repeat the activity using a pendulum 0.4 m long. Repeat Exercises 5–8 for the new data.

10. Repeat the activity using a pendulum 0.25 m long. Repeat Exercises 5–8 for the new data. Plot **L3** as x and **L4** as y. Is there a pattern? If so, is it linear or non-linear?

11. According to physics, the relationships between the length of a pendulum l and period T of one complete swing is $l = g\left(\dfrac{T}{2\pi}\right)^2$ where l is in meters, T is in seconds, and g is the acceleration due to the Earth's gravity, or 9.81 m/s^2. Write this equation in terms of x and y instead of T and l. Graph your equation on the same screen as the scatter plot from Exercise 10. Does this equation appear to be a good model? Explain.

12. Use this model to predict T when l = 0.75 m. Run the activity again with a string of length 0.75 m. Do you expect the exact answer? Explain.

13. Use your model to predict l when T = 1.6 s. Run the activity again with a string having the same length as your prediction. Was your prediction reasonable?

14. The model that was given had the period T as the independent variable. Rewrite the equation in terms of the length l. Does it make more sense to have the length as the independent or dependent variable? Explain your answer.

15. Make a pendulum 2 m long and suspend it from the ceiling of the classroom. Use the model to predict the duration of one period. Time the length of ten complete swings with a stopwatch. Divide the result by ten. Does the model give a reasonable prediction?

16. You can adjust a clock run by a pendulum by changing the length of the pendulum. If a clock runs slow, how should you adjust the pendulum?

Charge It! Activity 8

Set-up

Connect the TI Voltage Probe to Channel 1 of the CBL 2 unit. Connect the negative wire of the capacitor to the negative terminal of the battery. Attach the black voltage probe lead to the negative capacitor wire. Twist the positive capacitor wire with the end of one resistor wire. Connect the other resistor wire to the positive terminal of the battery. Attach the red voltage probe lead to the resistor wire that is attached to the battery. Have one student use the calculator. Another student should hold the 9 volt battery upright and a third student should hold the assembled electronic circuit.

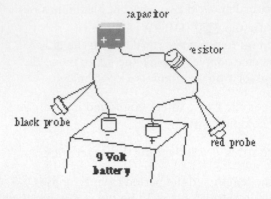

What You'll Learn
- Modeling exponential growth and decay

- Writing exponential equations

What You'll Need
CBL 2™ unit, graphing calculator compatible with CBL 2, TI Voltage Probe, needle-nose pliers, 220 microfarad (MFD) capacitor, 100 Ohm (Ω) resistor, 9 volt battery

Time Graph Settings (Mode: Time Graph–8)

- Time Interval = 0.08

- Number of Samples = 100

Channel Settings

- CH 1: VOLTAGE (V)

Pre-Activity Questions

1. The graphs to the right are examples of exponential functions. Which graph shows exponential growth? exponential decay?

2. An exponential function can be written in the form $y = ab^x$. Define the constants a and b.

3. In $f(x)$, is $b > 1$ or $0 < b < 1$? What about in $g(x)$?

4. What is the starting value of $f(x)$? What is the ratio between each adjacent y-value in the table? Write the equation of $f(x)$.

5. What is the starting value of $g(x)$? What is the ratio between each adjacent y-value in the table? Write the equation of $g(x)$.

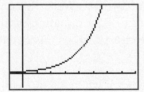

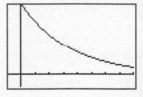

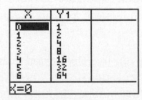

Activity

The student holding the circuit should touch the free wire of the resistor to the positive terminal of the battery and the negative wire of the capacitor to the negative terminal of the battery. Wait about 5 s. Run the DATAMATE program. Press **2 : START** on the calculator and wait for the second set of two beeps to separate the battery and the circuit.

Charge It! (continued)

6. Sketch the graph from the calculator screen on a graph like the one at right.

```
VOLTAGE(U)
|
|
|
|
|_____
              TIME(S)
```

7. Attach the red lead of the positive terminal of the 9 volt battery. Attach the black lead to the negative terminal. The voltage of the battery is displayed in the top right corner of the DATAMATE main screen. Record this voltage.

A capacitor stores electrical charge. The voltage of a capacitor is raised by the battery. After the capacitor is disconnected from the battery, the voltage drops rapidly but levels off. The resistor controls the rate of discharge. The voltage of the capacitor over time can be modeled by an exponential equation.

8. Press **TRACE** to find the y-intercept of the graph. What is the real-world significance of this value?

9. Compare the value of the y-intercept you found in Exercise 8 with your measurement in Exercise 7. Explain any difference.

10. The model equation of a discharging capacitor is $y = Ve^{-Kx}$. The general form of an exponential equation is $y = ab^x$. b is the base and e is a base that is used for the natural logarithm. a is the initial value of the function, or the y-intercept. How does a compare with V?

11. Why is the negative exponent in the model equation?

12. Use **TRACE** to find the voltage after 2 s; after 3 s.

13. After how many seconds does the voltage appear to level off?

14. Use the exponential regression option located in the CURVE FIT submenu of the ANALYZE menu to find a model for the data. Record the values of a and b.

15. Press **ENTER** to graph this function on the same graph as the data. How well does your graph match the data?

16. How does the value of a compare with the y-intercept of the data?

17. Does the model of the voltage ever reach zero? Is this reasonable?

18. Remember that the model equation of a discharging capacitor is $y = Ve^{-Kx}$. The value of b you found should compare to the value of e^{-K} from the model. In this case, $K = \dfrac{1}{0.022}$. Find e^{-K} and compare its value to b.

Falling Objects

Activity 9

Set-up

Place the motion detector face up on the floor. Use four textbooks to build two stacks on either side of the detector to protect it. Have a tall student stand on a chair and hold a smaller book steady over the detector. Make sure that the book will land on the textbooks and not on the motion detector. Two more students control the CBL 2 unit and a graphing calculator.

What You'll Learn
- Solving a system with three variables
- Finding points on a parabola
- Modeling data with a quadratic equation

What You'll Need
CBL 2™ unit, graphing calculator compatible with CBL 2, motion detector, five books

Time Graph Settings (Mode: Time Graph–1.6)

- Time Interval = 0.02
- Number of Samples = 80

Channel Settings

- DIG: MOTION (FT)

Pre-Activity Questions

1. Sketch a graph of the height of a falling book with respect to time.

2. Predict the type of equation that gives the best model for the motion of a falling object.

Activity

Begin by having one student run the program DATAMATE. The student presses **2 : START** on the TI-83/TI-83 Plus and the book-holder waits to hear the second set of two beeps. The book-holder should hold the book motionless over the detector for a short time after the motion detector starts collecting data to record the initial height of the book. When finished, link the data (located in **L1** and **L6**) to the rest of the class.

3. Sketch the graph of the data from the calculator on a graph like the one at the right. Explain the real-world significance of each section of the graph.

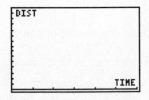

4. Use **TRACE** to select three points from the plot of data. Make sure they lie on the curve of the fall, not on either horizontal line.

5. The fall of an object is modeled well by a quadratic equation. Substitute each point you chose in Exercise 4 into the general equation for a quadratic function, $y = ax^2 + bx + c$. Round your answers to two decimal places.

6. Now you have a system with three variables. Use one of the matrix methods discussed in the textbook to solve the problem for a, b, and c. Round your answers to two decimal places.

Falling Objects (continued)

●●●

7. Substitute a, b, and c into the general equation of a quadratic function.

8. The initial height of the book should be the vertex of the parabola. Use TRACE to find the initial height.

9. Enter your model as **Y1** on the **Y=** screen and graph it with the plot of data. Does your model fit the data well? Explain. Sketch your model and the data.

10. Use the **2nd** [CALC] **4 : maximum** option of the calculator to find the vertex of the parabola. Now write your equation in vertex form, $y = a(x - h)^2 + k$.

11. Does the y-coordinate of the vertex you found agree with your answer from Exercise 8 for the initial height of the book? If not, rewrite your equation using the initial height for k and replace your old equation in the calculator.

12. What is the real-world significance of the x- and y-coordinates of the vertex of the parabola?

13. What is a reasonable domain for your quadratic equation? Why?

14. At what time was the book 2 feet from the floor? Solve either algebraically or on the graphing calculator.

15. From physics we know that the height of a falling object is modeled by the equation $h(t) = -16t^2 + h_0$. In this model t is the time in seconds since the object started to fall and h_0 is the initial height in feet of the object. This model assumes that the object was dropped with no initial velocity, and it neglects air resistance. Compare your model with the physics model. Do they agree? If not, explain.

●●●

Bouncing Ball, Part 1   Activity 10

Set-up

One student holds the motion detector 5 ft above and parallel to the floor (a clamp can also be used to hold the detector). A second student holds the ball with both hands about 1.5 ft below the motion detector. A third student runs the DATAMATE program. Be sure that the ball bounces on a smooth, level surface.

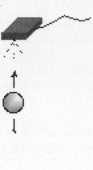

Time Graph Settings (Mode: Time Graph–4)

*   Time Interval = 0.04

*   Number of Samples = 100

Channel Settings

*   DIG: MOTION (FT)

Pre-Activity Questions

1. The ball will drop and bounce several times. On a graph like the one at right, sketch a graph of the distance between the ball and the motion detector.

2. In the activity that follows, you will invert the data collected by the CBL 2 so that height represents the distance to the floor, not the distance from the motion detector. Does this change what you expect to see? Explain your answer. Redraw the graph if necessary.

3. How high will the ball bounce each time? Will the ball bounce the same percent of the previous height each time? Explain.

Activity

Start the DATAMATE program. The student operating the calculator should press **2 : START.** Another student drops the ball after the second set of two beeps. If the ball bounces sideways away from the motion detector, repeat the activity. When you are satisfied with the data, exit the DATAMATE program. Enter the command 'max(L6) − L6 → L6' on the home screen. This will invert the data that represents height. Link all the calculators so that everyone has **L1** and **L6.**

4. Sketch a graph of the plot in an appropriate viewing window.

5. Select one bounce that forms a good parabola. Use **TRACE** to find the coordinates of the vertex of the parabola.

Bouncing Ball, Part 1 (continued)

6. Press **Y=** **CLEAR** and enter the equation $y = a(x - h)^2 + k$, using the coordinates of the vertex as (h, k) in the equation. The only variables should be x and a. How can you find the value of a? List as many ways as possible.

7. With **STO►** you can use Guess and Test to find a best value of a. To store 1 to a, press 1 **STO►** **ALPHA** **A** **ENTER**. Press **GRAPH** to see the model of the data. How good is your first guess?

8. Now store -1 to a by pressing -1 **STO►** **ALPHA** **A** **ENTER**. Compare the model with the data. What is the difference between a positive and negative value for a? Which sign models the bounce?

9. Store -4 to a and press **GRAPH**. How has the model changed? Describe the relationship between the value of A and the width of the parabola.

10. Keep guessing different values for a until you have a good fit. Write your model equation in vertex form, $y = a(x - h)^2 + k$. Compare your answer to others in your class. Explain any differences.

11. Is the vertex of a bounce always represented by a data point? If not, how does this affect the accuracy of your model?

12. Referring to your answers to Exercise 6, use another method to find the value of a. Compare this new model equation with your model equation from Exercise 10.

13. What is the real-world significance of each of the constants a, h, and k with respect to the physics of the ball? Which value should be almost the same for any bounce? Explain.

Bouncing Ball, Part 2

Activity 11

Set-up

One student holds the motion detector 5 ft above and parallel to the floor (a clamp can also be used to hold the detector). A second student holds the ball with both hands about 1.5 ft below the motion detector. A third student runs the DATAMATE program. Be sure that the ball bounces on a smooth, level surface.

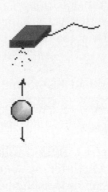

Time Graph Settings (Mode: Time Graph–4)

- Time Interval = 0.04

- Number of Samples = 100

Channel Settings

- DIG: MOTION (FT)

Pre-Activity Questions

1. The ball is going to be dropped and should bounce several times. Sketch a graph of its height with respect to time on a graph like the one at right.

2. Does the ball continue bouncing, or does it eventually come to a stop?

3. With each bounce, the ball rises slightly less than the previous bounce. Describe the difference between the maximum heights of consecutive bounces. Do the differences increase, decrease, or remain constant?

4. The maximum height of one bounce can be expressed as a percent of the maximum height of the previous bounce. Does this percent remain constant?

Activity

Start the DATAMATE program. The student operating the calculator should press **2 : START.** Another student drops the ball after the second set of two beeps. If the ball bounces sideways away from the motion detector, repeat the activity. When you are satisfied with the data, exit the DATAMATE program. Enter the command 'max(L6) − L6 → L6' on the home screen. This will invert the data that represents height. Link all the calculators so that everyone has **L1** and **L6.**

5. Sketch a graph of the data from the graphing calculator screen. How many complete bounces are there in the data? Do not count the initial fall of the ball.

6. Number each bounce from your graph from Exercise 5. Label the initial height as bounce zero.

What You'll Learn
- Finding the base of an exponential equation

- Modeling data with an exponential equation

What You'll Need
CBL 2™ unit, graphing calculator compatible with CBL 2, motion detector, racquetball or other non-fuzzy ball

Bouncing Ball, Part 2 (continued)

7. Use TRACE to find the vertex of each bounce. Make a table of the bounce number and the maximum height of each bounce. Include bounce zero and use the height of the ball before its release as its height.

8. Enter the data from the table in **L3** and **L4** on the calculator. Plot the data on the calculator and sketch a graph of the data from the table.

9. What type of functions could fit the data in your graph?

10. An exponential equation can be used to model the decrease in height of a bouncing ball. Why is a quadratic equation not used to model this data?

11. Use the general exponential equation $y = ab^x$ to write an equation to model this data. a is the initial height of the ball. Use TRACE to find a from your data.

12. b is the rebound percent of each bounce. Use the table in Exercise 7 to find the height of two adjacent bounces and solve for b.

13. Write your final equation.

14. Enter your equation as **Y1** on the calculator and graph it with the scatter plot. How well does your model fit the decrease in maximum heights? If it does not fit well, use different bounces to find a more accurate value for b.

15. Use your model to determine the maximum height of the 10th bounce.

16. Suppose the ball stops bouncing when its maximum height is less than 2 in. above the floor. Using your model, how many times does the ball bounce before it stops?

17. What is the scientific name for the rebound percent?

When's the Tea Ready?

Activity 12

Set-up

Plug the TI temperature probe into Channel 1 of the CBL 2 unit. Place the end of the probe into the hot water. The measurements are in °C.

Time Graph Settings (Mode: Time Graph–180)

- Time Interval = 5

- Number of Samples = 36

Channel Settings

- CH 1: TEMP(C)

Pre-Activity Questions

1. What is the highest temperature the water will reach during your class period? the lowest? Explain.

2. Sketch a graph representing the temperature of the water with respect to time on a graph like the one at right.

3. Suppose you record the temperature of the probe as it cools. Would its graph appear different from the graph of the cooling water? Explain.

Activity

Place the probe in the cup of hot water. Wait about a minute for the probe to reach the water's temperature. Run the program DATAMATE. Remove the probe from the water, wipe it dry quickly, and press **2 : START.** Place the probe so that it doesn't touch anything, but hangs freely in the air. The data is stored in **L1** and **L2.** When the program is done, link all the calculators to share the data.

4. With the temperature probe still attached to the CBL 2 unit, go to the main screen of the DATAMATE program and record the room temperature located in the top right corner of the screen.

5. Sketch the graph from the calculator screen.

6. What type of equations have a shape similar to your graph from Exercise 5?

7. Exponential equations can be written in the form $y = ab^x$. What is the horizontal asymptote for an exponential equation in this form?

8. Use the **2nd** [DRAW] feature to approximate the horizontal asymptote of the data. Is your answer consistent with your answer from Exercise 7?

9. Would the equation $y = ab^x + c$ provide a more realistic model? Explain.

10. What value should c have in your model equation? What is the real-world significance of c?

> ### What You'll Learn
> - Modeling exponential data
>
> - Translating exponential equations
>
> ### What You'll Need
> CBL 2™ unit, graphing calculator compatible with CBL 2, TI temperature probe, insulated cup or mug, source of hot water

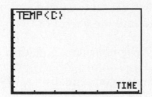

When's the Tea Ready? (continued)

11. Temperature data is recorded in **L2** and time is recorded in **L1**. It is useful to adjust the data so that the asymptote is the *x*-axis. Use the arrow keys to move the cursor bar to the top of list **L3**. Press **2nd** [L2] **−**. Then enter the value of *c* and press **ENTER**. The sample screen to the right shows a room temperature of 22.1°C.

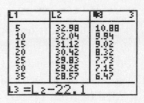

12. Now change **Plot1** to use **L1** and **L3** instead of **L1** and **L2.** For a better view of the graph use the **ZOOM** **9 : ZoomStat** option.

13. Now use the exponential regression (**ExpReg**) option from the **STAT** CALC menu to find a model for the cooling of the water. Choose the correct lists by entering **L1, L3.** Write the equation of your exponential model. Round your answers for *a* and *b* to four decimal places.

14. Use the regression equation (**RegEQ**) option of the **VARS** feature to enter your model as Y1. Then press **GRAPH** to view your model on top of the scatter plot. Does the model fit the data well? Explain.

15. Add the value of *c* you found in Exercise 10 to your equation from Exercise 13. Write down the complete model equation.

16. Is *a* the initial temperature of the probe? Explain.

17. Graph the complete model with a plot of the original data in lists **L1** and **L2.** Explain how this model relates to the model you graphed in Exercise 14?

Reheat the water and perform the activity again. Leave the temperature probe in the water and enter 60 for the Time Interval. This time you are measuring the temperature of the water as it cools. The program runs for 36 min. If you are satisfied with the data, link to the other calculators in the class.

18. Sketch the graph from the calculator screen. Does the scatter plot have a shape that is similar to the first plot? Will the temperature of any cooling have a similar shape?

19. Will an exponential equation model this set of data as well? any data of a cooling object?

20. Follow the steps in Exercises 8 and 11–15 to write a model for the data of the cooling water.

21. According to the model, at what time would the water reach 45°C?

22. Suppose that the water was boiling when the temperature was first measured. What would be the value of *a* for this model? What about *b* and *c*? Explain. How long would it take the boiling water to cool to 45°C?

Full Speed Ahead

Activity 13

Set-up

Place a motion detector on top of a couple of books facing into an open path into the room. You are going to run a toy car away from the motion detector. You will need a spring-loaded or wind-up car.

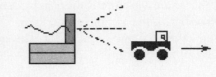

Time Graph Settings (Mode: Time Graph–1.6)

- Time Interval = 0.02

- Number of Samples = 80

Channel Settings

- DIG: MOTION (FT)

Pre-Activity Questions

1. Sketch the graph of a car moving at a constant speed on a graph like the one at right.

2. Sketch the graph of a car that is speeding up on the same graph.

3. Sketch the graph of a car that is slowing down on the same graph.

> ### What You'll Learn
> - Writing quadratic equations to model data
>
> - Solving systems of quadratic equations
>
> - Using a model to make predictions
>
> ### What You'll Need
> CBL 2™ unit, graphing calculator compatible with CBL 2, motion detector, wind-up car

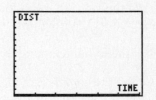

Activity

Place the wind-up car about 1.5 ft away from the motion detector, facing away from the detector. Have a student run the program DATAMATE and press **2 : START.** Start the car after the second set of two beeps. Link the data (located in **L1** and **L6**) to the other students in the class.

4. Sketch the plot from the calculator. Does the data appear to be linear?

5. Find a linear equation to model the motion of the car. What is the significance of the slope and the *y*-intercept of the car?

6. Graph your model on the graphing calculator along with the plot of the data. How well does the model fit the data? If you have studied residuals, do a residual plot and use the results in your answer.

7. Do you think that the data should be linear or quadratic? Explain with respect to the motion of the car.

8. Find a quadratic model for the data.

9. Graph your model on the graphing calculator. How well does the model fit the data? If you have studied residuals, do a residual plot and use the results in your answer.

Full Speed Ahead (continued)

10. A quadratic model means that the speed of the car was either increasing or decreasing. Does your model indicate an increasing, decreasing, or constant speed? Explain how you can tell from the graph.

11. Sketch a graph representing the motion of the wind-up car from start to stop. Explain your answer.

12. Why does the data collected by the CBL 2 not match your expectations? Discuss a reasonable domain for your model.

Repeat the activity. This time set the Time Interval as 0.06 and the Number of Samples as 120. Be sure that the car starts from the same location. When you are finished, link the data to the other students in the class.

13. Sketch the data that was collected using these new settings. Label what is happening at each time on the graph.

Use **Select(** to separate the data into two sets, the initial acceleration and the final deceleration. You can also select three points from each section and store them as data lists.

14. Find a quadratic equation to model the car's acceleration. Graph this model with the data. How well does your equation model the first part of the data?

15. Find a quadratic equation to model the car's deceleration. Graph this model with the data and your model from Exercise 14. How well does your second equation model the second part of the data?

16. How could you find when the car started to slow? Give two methods, one graphic and one algebraic. Use both methods to find this point.

In the Swing of Things

Activity 14

Set-up

Place two tables less than 1 m apart in a clear area in your classroom. Stack books on each table so that the top of each stack is more than 1 m from the floor. Bridge the two stacks with a meter stick. Place additional books on the meter stick to hold it in place. Attach a piece of string to a non-fuzzy ball like a racquetball. Hang the string from the center of the meter stick. Set the motion detector on a stack of books so that the grill has the same height as the resting ball. The detector must be at least 0.5 m from the ball when the ball is pulled toward the detector at a 20° angle.

Front View

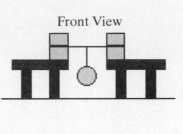

Side View

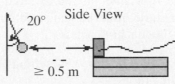

What You'll Learn
- Using trigonometric equations in a real-world situation

- Finding values to fit a cosine equation

- Modeling data with trigonometric equations

What You'll Need
CBL 2™ unit, graphing calculator compatible with CBL 2, motion detector, at least 2 m of string, racquetball or other non-fuzzy ball, meter stick, means to suspend pendulum

Time Graph Settings (Mode: Time Graph–2)

- Time Interval = 0.02

- Number of Samples = 100

Channel Settings

- DIG: MOTION (FT)

Pre-Activity Questions

1. Imagine you are observing a pendulum swinging back and forth. Sketch a graph of its back-and-forth motion on a graph like the one at right.

2. Which factors affect the length of time each swing takes?

3. What type of function does your graph resemble?

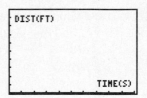

Activity

Use a length of string between 0.25 m and 0.75 m. Check that the motion detector is at the same height as the ball. Start the program DATAMATE. Pull the ball back at a 20° angle toward the motion detector. Have a student press **2 : START** while the other student releases the ball after the second set to two beeps. When finished, link that data (located in **L1** and **L6**) to the other members of the class.

4. This real-world problem can be modeled by a cosine function. The general form of a cosine function is $y = a\cos b(x - c) + d$. Write what each variable represents.

5. Use TRACE to find the coordinates of the first peak of the graph. From the home screen press X,T,θ,n STO▶ ALPHA L ENTER to save the x-coordinate. Press GRAPH and use TRACE to save the y-coordinate as **M** in a similar manner. The ordered pair **L, M** represents the first maximum of the graph.

In the Swing of Things (continued)

6. Now TRACE to the first minimum. Store the coordinates as the ordered pair **N, O.**

7. Finally, TRACE to the second maximum. Store the coordinates of the second maximum as the ordered pair **P, Q.**

8. How can you find the amplitude of a periodic function? Use the three ordered pairs to find the amplitude of the pendulum's swing. Store this value as the variable **A** in the calculator.

9. How can you find the period of the pendulum's swing? Use the three ordered pairs to find the period. This number is equal to $\frac{2\pi}{b}$. Solve for b and store the value as the variable **B.**

10. How can you find the horizontal translation of a cosine function? Use the three ordered pairs to find c and store the value as the variable **C.**

11. How can you find the vertical translation of the graph? Find the vertical translation and store the value as **D.**

12. Use the four values you just found to enter the model cosine function in the form $y = a\cos b(x - c) + d$ as **Y1** in the Y= screen.

13. Press GRAPH to see the model and the plot of the pendulum's motion. You may need to adjust the vertical shift, d. Once you have achieved a good fit, write the equation you found.

14. Run the experiment with the same length of string, but this time pull the ball farther back. What values in the cosine equation does this change? Explain.

15. Change the length of the string and run the experiment again. Find a new model. What values in the cosine equation does this change? Explain.

16. Explain how the variables in the general equation $y = a\cos b(x - c) + d$ relate to the physical setup of the pendulum.

Playing With Numbers

Activity 15

In this activity you will learn some interesting facts about numbers. You will also see how a calculator can facilitate explorations involving large numbers. In addition, you will formulate some conjectures related to your investigations and work towards the idea of writing a mathematical proof to verify these conjectures.

Investigate

1. Store the number 123456789 in your calculator as the variable A.

2. Use the command '2A' to multiply this number by 2. What do you notice about the digits of this product?

3. Multiply A by 4. What do you notice about the digits of this product?

4. Multiply A by 5, 7, and 8. What do you notice about the digits of these products?

5. Multiply A by 10, 11, 13, 14, 16, 17, and 20. What do you notice about the digits of these products? Has anything changed from the previous set of multiples?

6. Notice that some multiples of A behave differently, so those have been omitted from our list. What do all these multiples (with the exception of 19A) have in common?

7. Based on your answer to Exercise 6, predict the next 4 multiples of 123456789 that will behave in a similar manner. Test your prediction with the calculator.

8. What happens when you find the same multiples for 987654321?

Investigate

1. Use your calculator to find the squares of 11, 111, and 1111.

2. Make a conjecture about what will happen when you square 11111. Test your conjecture.

3. Find the squares of 11, 111, and 1111 using paper and pencil. How does this approach help you explain the pattern in the square of these numbers?

4. Find the squares of 111111 and 1111111. Your calculator will most likely express these numbers in scientific notation. Explain why you can still observe the pattern found in Exercises 1 and 2.

5. The square of 11111111 is shown in the screen at right. Looking at the last seven, it appears that the pattern breaks down, although this is not actually true. Explain.

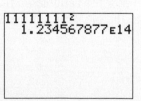

6. Explain why the pattern does eventually break down when you square 1111111111. A paper and pencil approach may once again help with your explanation.

Playing With Numbers (continued)

Investigate

1. Write down any integer with several digits.

2. Form a different number by writing the digits of your first number in a different order.

3. Use your calculator to subtract the smaller of your two numbers from the larger.

4. Add the digits of your answer together. If this sum is a one-digit number, leave it alone. Otherwise, take this number and repeat Exercises 2 through 4 until you obtain a one-digit sum. What is this sum?

5. Repeat Exercises 1 through 4 using a different number. You will always end up with the same one-digit sum. What is this sum?

6. **Writing** The interesting result found in Exercise 5 can be *proved* using algebra, which uses variables in place of numbers. Explain why it is necessary to use variables rather than specific numbers when writing a mathematical proof.

Exercises

1. What happens when you multiply any two-digit number by 101010101?

2. What happens when you divide the numbers 1 through 8 by 9? Do the resulting decimals terminate or keep on repeating?

3. Does the pattern observed in Exercise 2 continue when you divide 9 by 9? Explain.

4. Try dividing numbers from 1 to 98 by 99. Explain the pattern you observe.

5. Does the pattern observed in Exercise 4 continue when you divide 99 by 99? Explain.

Finding Real Roots of Equations   Activity 16

The early history of algebra was dominated by the quest to find real number roots of equations, a topic that comes up many times in mathematics courses. The purpose of this exploration is to show you three different methods by which you can solve virtually *any* equation with a graphing calculator—a capability that would have dazzled the great mathematicians of the past if they had lived to see it. The technology does not render their algebraic discoveries obsolete (indeed, those discoveries made the technology possible), but it does affect the motivation for studying algebra. Modern students can spend more time learning *how* it works and *why* it works without worrying as much about *making* it work.

We will use three different methods to find the real roots of the equation $x^2 = \cos(x)$, an equation for which a pencil-and-paper algebraic does not exist. Don't worry if you have never seen $\cos(x)$ before; all that matters is that it is a function and your calculator will graph it.

Investigate

Before entering the equations, press MODE and verify that the third line has 'Radian' highlighted. If not, place the cursor over 'Radian' and press ENTER.

1. Enter the functions $y = x^2$ and $y = \cos(x)$ as Y1 and Y2 on on your calculator. Press ZOOM **4 : ZDecimal** to graph them in the 'Zdecimal' window. You should get screen shown at right.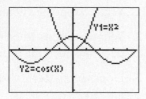

2. In the [2nd] [CALC] menu, choose 'intersect' to find where the graphs intersect. The calculator will ask 'First Curve?' with its cursor located on the graph of Y1. That's one of the curves you want, so press ENTER. Press ENTER again to choose the graph of Y2 as the second curve.

3. When the calculator prompts 'Guess?', it wants to be given an *x*-coordinate close to the desired intersection point. You can either move the cursor toward one of the intersection points (as shown on the first screen below) or enter a reasonable guess, such as 1 (as shown on the second screen below). In either case, the calculator will locate the *x* and *y*-coordinates of the intersection point nearest to your guess. As seen in the third screen below, the *x*-coordinate, .82413231, represents the first solution to the equation $x^2 = \cos(x)$.

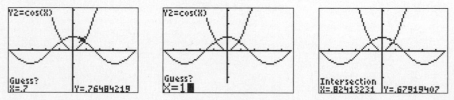

4. Return to the home screen and press X,T,θ,*n* ENTER. This will give you the positive solution to the equation $x^2 = \cos(x)$ to even more decimal places.

5. Using symmetry of the graph, predict the negative solution without performing any more calculations. Check your solution using the 'intersect' feature of your graphing calculator.

Investigate

You will now solve the same equation by setting the equation $x^2 = \cos(x)$ equal to zero and using the 'Zero' feature of your calculator.

Finding Real Roots of Equations (continued)

6. Enter the function $y = x^2 - \cos(x)$ as Y1 and graph it in the same ZDecimal window. Press **2nd** [CALC] **2 : zero** to find the zeros of the function. Since the calculator can only find one zero at a time, it will ask for a 'left bound' (any number slightly to the left of one of the x-intercepts) and a 'right bound' (any number slightly to the right). Your two bounds should capture exactly one of the x-intercepts between them. Then enter a reasonable guess. The calculator will find the zero of the function closest to your guess.

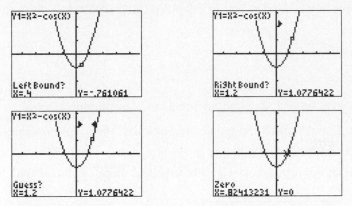

7. Repeat the procedure described in Exercise 6 to find the negative solution.

Investigate

Here's a third way to solve $x^2 = \cos(x)$.

1. Press **MATH** **0 : Solver** to open the 'Solver'. Type in the equation. If that function is still stored as Y1 you can simply enter Y1 (press **VARS** **▶** Y-VARS **1 : Function 1 : Y1**). If an equation is already displayed at the top of the screen, press the up arrow and type in the correct equation.

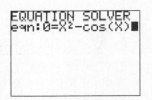

2. Press **ENTER** and type '1' next to 'X=' to indicate a guess that is close to the zero you want to find first. Press **ALPHA** [SOLVE] to instruct the calculator to find the zero of $x^2 - \cos(x) = 0$ closest to your guess.

3. Repeat the procedure described in Exercise 2 to find the negative solution.

Exercises

1. The two real roots of the equation $x^2 - \cos(x) = 0$ are irrational numbers. Explain what this means about the calculator solutions found in this exploration.

2. Use each of the three methods described in this activity to find the two real solutions of the equation $(x - 1)^2 = \sin(x)$.

3. **Writing** Some equations have solutions that are not real numbers. Explain why the graphical methods in this exploration can only find real number solutions.

Solving Absolute Value Inequalities Graphically

Activity 17

The absolute value function is an interesting function. Its main use in mathematics is to provide a way of expressing algebraic distances, but it also shows up in equations and inequalities that must be solved. In many cases, an algebraic solution of an absolute value inequality can be quite difficult to find. For example, the paper and pencil solution to $|x - 1| + |3x - 4| < |1 - 2x|$ is extremely difficult to carry out. On the other hand, geometric solutions are possible in a number of ways. You will explore three such solutions in the following activity.

Investigate

You will first solve the inequality $|x - 1| \leq 2$ by the intersection of graphs method.

1. Enter 'abs(X − 1)' and '2' as Y1 and Y2, respectively. Note that the absolute value function is located in the **MATH** NUM menu.

2. Graph both functions in an appropriate window (In this case, **ZOOM** **4 : ZDecimal** works well).

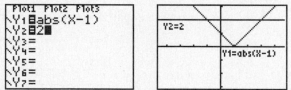

3. Observe that the function Y1 is less than Y2 where the V dips below the horizontal line $y = 2$. This happens in the x-interval $[-1, 3]$. Locate the endpoints of this interval by using the 'intersect' command (**2nd** [CALC]). You can check that the endpoints are correct by replacing x with -1 and 3 in the original inequality and verifying that the left side equals 2.

Investigate

This time you will solve the same inequality, $|x - 1| \leq 2$, by considering the inequality $|x - 1| - 2 \leq 0$.

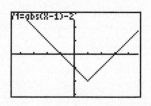

4. Enter the single function $|x - 1| - 2$ as Y1 in your calculator and graph it in the same window as before.

5. Explain how the solution $[-1, 3]$ can be found by looking at this graph.

6. Explain how you would identify the solution to $|x - 1| - 2 \geq 0$ by observing the same graph.

Solving Absolute Value Inequalities
Graphically (continued)

Investigate

Here's a way to instruct the calculator to reveal the solution to $|x - 1| \leq 2$ as a
line graph.

7. Press **MODE** and change 'Connected' to 'Dot' on the fifth
   line. This time enter *the inequality itself* as Y1 and graph it
   in the same window you have been using (The $\leq$ sign is in
   the **2nd** [TEST] menu.). You will get the graph at right.

8. Since the function you entered as Y1 is a *statement* rather than an *expression*, it is
   interpreted by the calculator as a *truth function*. A value of 1 is returned when the
   statement is true and a value of 0 is returned when the statement is false. Explain
   why this truth function will produce the graph shown in Exercise 7.

Exercises

1. Solve the inequality $|2x + 1| \leq 3$ graphically using each of the methods described
   in the investigations. Which method do you prefer? Why?

2. Choose one method to solve $|7x - 2| < 3$.

3. Solve $|2x - 4| < |x| - 1$ using any graphical method.

4. **Challenge** Solve the inequality $|x - 1| + |3x - 4| < |1 - 2x|$. You may solve it
   graphically or, as an extra challenge, algebraically.

Magic Pricing Numbers

Activity 18

Dickie's Discount Draperies buys caseloads of draperies at wholesale prices and sells them individually to consumers at discount rates. Here is the procedure Dickie followed to arrive at his "sale price" for each pair of drapes from a case that cost $412.56 wholesale.

Step 1 Since there are 24 pairs of drapes in the case, he divided the case price by 24.

Step 2 He took the individual wholesale price and increased it by 16% to get a starting retail price.

Step 3 He marked the starting retail price down by 10% to get his discount sale price.

Step 4 He tacked on an affiliated member surcharge of 2.8%.

Step 5 He rounded up to the next whole cent.

Dickie went through the same elaborate process for another case that cost $644.20. Then he did it again for another case, and so on. Even with a calculator, this was tedious work. Then Dickie's stockboy saw him working one day and offered to show him how to find his sale price as a *function* of the wholesale case price, enabling him to price his drapes with a single operation. The stockboy said he would use some algebra he had learned in school. Dickie was skeptical.

Investigate

1. Suppose x is the wholesale case price. By what number can Dickie multiply x to get the wholesale price of a single pair of drapes?

2. By what number can he multiply the wholesale price in order to increase it by 16%?

3. By what number can he multiply this starting retail price in order to discount it by 10%?

4. By what number can he multiply this discounted price in order to add on the 2.8% surcharge?

5. By what number can Dickie multiply his wholesale case price x in order to effect all of these operations at once?

6. Write the final (unrounded) discounted sale price y as a function of the wholesale case price x. Enter it as Y1 in your calculator.

In the NUM submenu of the MATH menu, there is a command that will round a number to a specified number of decimal places. Specifically, the command 'round(Y1, 2)' will round Y1 to 2 decimal places.

7. Explain why the command 'round(Y1+.005, 2)' will always round Y1 *up* to the next whole cent.

Enter the function 'round(Y1+.005, 2)' as Y2 in your calculator and turn off Y1 by placing the cursor over the '=' sign and pressing ENTER. Press 2nd [TBLSET] and change 'Indpnt' (the independent variable) from 'Auto' to 'Ask'. Now press 2nd [TABLE].

8. Enter the wholesale case price, 412.56, in the X column and press ENTER. Is the value in the Y2 column consistent with the answer found earlier?

Magic Pricing Numbers (continued)

9. Find the discount retail price of a single pair of drapes for the $644.20 case.

The stockboy was immediately given a $10-per-hour raise and named assistant manager of the store. The next day he sent flowers to his algebra teacher.

Exercises

1. Find the discounted price of a pair of drapes from a case of 24 costing $483.46 wholesale.

2. Suppose Dickie has a case of 36 pairs of drapes that cost him $857.98 wholesale. Show how he can easily adjust his function to find the individual discount price for a pair of drapes from this larger case.

3. Write a function that will give the wholesale case price for a case of 24 drapes as a function of the discounted retail price x.

Mrs. Murphy's Algebra Test Scores   Activity 19

Mrs. Murphy's algebra class did very well on her first major test, with scores ranging from a low of 78 to a high of 98. Inspired by their success, she decided to make up a much more challenging second test in order to see just how good her students were. Unfortunately, she made the test *too* hard, even for her top students, and their scores on the harder test only ranged from a low of 42 to a high of 72. Not wishing to punish her students for her own misjudgment of their abilities, Mrs. Murphy decided to scale the grades to match the range of scores on her first test.

Here's how she did it. She drew a line segment to represent the range of raw scores on the second test:

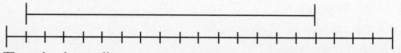

Then she drew a line segment to represent the range of scores where she wanted her scaled score to fall.

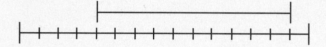

Using the diagrams above, you can determine an appropriate scale.

Investigate

1. Determine the length of each line.

2. Consider a point *x* on the first line that represents a student's raw score on the second test. In terms of *x*, write an expression that represents the distance from *x* to the left side of the first line.

3. What is the ratio of the distance found in Exercise 2 to the entire length of the line?

4. Repeat Exercises 2 and 3 for a point *y* on the second line.

5. Write a proportion that equates the ratios found in Exercises 3 and 4.

Solve this equation for *y* and write the resulting formula as Y1 in the 'Y=' editor of your calculator. Press MODE and change the second line from 'FLOAT' to '0'. Set the window to Xmin = 40, Xmax = 80, Xscl = 5, Ymin = 76, Ymax = 100, Yscl = 5 and graph the function.

6. What is the shape of the function you just graphed?

Use TRACE to see how the raw scores (X) are converted to scaled scores (Y). You can also see the curved scores in a table. Press 2nd [TBLSET] and set up a table as shown in the screen at right. Then press 2nd [TABLE] and see the scaled scores displayed next to the raw scores.

Mrs. Murphy's Algebra Test Scores (continued)

Exercises

1. What score on Mrs. Murphy's second test will be converted to 90?

2. Suppose the lowest score on the second test had been 32 rather than 42. How would this have affected Mrs. Murphy's scaling formula?

3. Write a formula that will convert scores that range from 40 to 76 to grades that range from 72 to 99.

Exploring Point-Slope Form   Activity 20

While *slope-intercept* form is convenient for graphing linear equations by hand, it is often easier to work with linear equations in *point-slope* form. You have learned that a line that passes through the point (h, k) with slope m has an equation that can be written in point-slope form as

$$y - k = m(x - h).$$

To enter this into your calculator, all you need to do is move k to the other side:

$$y = m(x - h) + k.$$

Investigate

1. Find the equation of the line in point-slope form that goes through $(2, 1)$ and has slope 3. Enter the equation in the calculator and use the "square" window shown at right.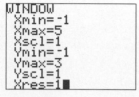

2. To highlight the point $(2, 1)$, store the coordinates in L1 and L2 as shown, using the curly brackets.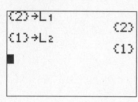

3. Next, press **2nd** [STATPLOT] and **ENTER**. Set up Plot 1 as shown in the screen below. Press **ENTER** to see the line with slope 3 passing through $(2, 1)$.

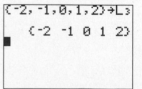 

4. Now graph several lines through $(2, 1)$ having different slopes. Store the slopes $\{0, \pm 1, \pm 2\}$ in list L3 and use L3 as the slope of the line, as shown below. (Notice the use of the multiplication sign in the second screen. A list followed directly by a parenthesis has a special meaning and is not interpreted by the graphing calculator as multiplication.)

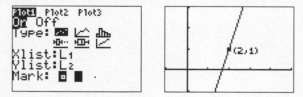

5. **Challenge** Add two numbers to the list L3 to produce the graph shown at right.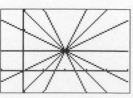

Exploring Point-Slope Form (continued)

Exercises

1. Produce a graph of a line through the point $(-5, 6)$ with slope -2.

2. Produce a graph of four different lines through $(-5, 6)$.

3. Produce a graph of two perpendicular lines intersecting at $(4, 9)$.

4. Produce a graph of four different lines with *x*-intercept 3.

5. Produce a graph through $(12, 12)$ that looks like the one shown at right. (*Hint*: You can fool the graphing calculator into showing a vertical line by making the slope very steep.)

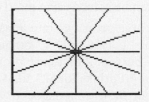

Fast Food Follies

Activity 21

· ·

It is hard to believe how many complicated problems in real life can be reduced to systems of simultaneous linear equations. The 19th century development of matrix algebra offered a systematic approach for solving these often complicated systems. While matrices simplified the arithmetic involved in solving complicated systems, the potential for computational error was still quite great. It wasn't until the arrival of today's matrix algebra programs, which are available in hand-held calculators, that the full potential of matrix algebra was realized. Below is a typical real-life problem that can be solved using matrix algebra.

Three people go into a fast food restaurant to pick up orders for their offices. The first person orders 3 burgers, 4 fries, and 4 soft drinks for $16.45. The second orders 5 burgers, 2 fries, and 5 soft drinks for $19.30. The third orders 4 burgers, 6 fries, and 6 soft drinks for $23.50. What are the individual prices the restaurant charges for a burger, fries, and a coke?

Investigate

1. Write the given information as a system of three linear equations in x, y, and z, where x is the cost of a burger, y is the cost of an order of fries, and z is the cost of a soft drink.

2. Explain why this system can be written as a single matrix equation

$$\begin{bmatrix} 3 & 4 & 4 \\ 5 & 2 & 5 \\ 4 & 6 & 6 \end{bmatrix} \begin{bmatrix} x \\ y \\ z \end{bmatrix} = \begin{bmatrix} 16.45 \\ 19.30 \\ 23.50 \end{bmatrix}$$, which is of the form $AX = B$.

$\underset{A}{\uparrow} \quad \underset{X}{\uparrow} \quad \underset{B}{\uparrow}$

3. Explain why the matrix expression $\begin{bmatrix} 3 & 4 & 4 \\ 5 & 2 & 5 \\ 4 & 6 & 6 \end{bmatrix}^{-1} \begin{bmatrix} 16.45 \\ 19.30 \\ 23.50 \end{bmatrix}$ solves this system.

4. The values of x, y, and z can be found by entering matrices A and B in the calculator. To edit matrix A, press **2nd** [MATRX] (*Note*: on the TI-83 just press **MATRX**), place the cursor over EDIT, and press **ENTER** . Enter matrix [A] as seen in the screen on the left below. Matrix B can be entered by pressing **2nd** [MATRX], placing the cursor over EDIT, then pressing **2** **ENTER** .

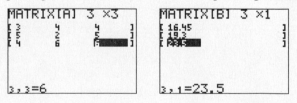

Fast Food Follies (continued)

5. Press **2nd** [QUIT] to return to the home screen and type **2nd** [MATRX] **ENTER** **x⁻¹** **2nd** [MATRX] **2** **ENTER** to obtain the screen at right. The calculator will produce the matrix of answers x, y, and z reading from top to bottom.

```
[A]⁻¹[B]
          [[2.35]
           [1.4 ]
           [.95 ]]
■
```

The result from Exercise 5 shows that each burger costs $2.35, each order of fries costs $1.40, and each soft drink costs $.95.

6. Suppose the town has a 7% sales tax on restaurant food, bringing the totals to $17.60, $20.65, and $25.15. How can we recover the original costs? This is a job for *scalar multiplication*. Enter the new matrix as [C]; then return to the home screen. We wish to reverse the effect of multiplying by 1.07 and rounding, which means we divide by 1.07 and round to 2 decimal places (nearest penny).

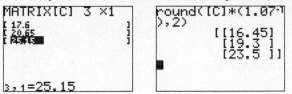

```
MATRIX[C] 3 ×1
[ 17.6      ]
[ 20.65     ]
[ 25.15     ]


3,1=25.15
```

```
round([C]*(1.07⁻¹
),2)
          [[16.45]
           [19.3 ]
           [23.5 ]]

■
```

Notice that we multiply by 1.07^{-1} rather than divide by 1.07. There is no such operation as *scalar division* on your calculator.

Exercises

Suppose three people walk into another restaurant that charges a 7% sales tax. The first person orders 3 burgers, 5 fries, and 5 soft drinks for $24.98. The second person orders 4 burgers, 4 fries, and 4 soft drinks for $25.04. The third person orders 4 burgers, 5 fries, and 6 soft drinks for $29.32. *All these totals include tax.*

1. Edit matrix [A] to represent the number of burgers, fries, and soft drinks ordered by each person.

2. Edit matrix [B] to represent the total, including tax, of each order.

3. Use scalar multiplication with matrix [B] to determine the total cost of each order, excluding tax and rounded to the nearest penny. Press **STO▶** **2nd** [MATRX] **3** to store this answer as matrix [C].

4. Use matrices [A] and [C] to determine the individual menu prices for a burger, fries, and a soft drink at this other restaurant.

5. In light of the second person's order, explain why the first person could not possibly have ordered 2 burgers, 2 fries, and 2 soft drinks at this restaurant for $10.50. Change matrices [A] and [B] to reflect this "impossible" order. What happens when you attempt to answer Exercises 3 and 4 with this new information? Do you get a solution?

Wheat on a Chessboard   Activity 22

Once upon a time, a peasant saved a traveling stranger from a thief who was about to kill him for his money. The stranger turned out to be the king, who gratefully promised to repay the peasant with anything he desired (within reason) from the wealth of his kingdom. The peasant, a clever fellow, made this simple request: a common chessboard with a single grain of wheat on the first square, two grains of wheat on the second, four on the third, eight on the fourth, and so on up to the 64th square. The king declared this request to be very reasonable and so ordered his minister of wheat to carry it out.

Before long the nervous wheat minister came to the king to report that the kingdom was completely out of wheat. Moreover, he added, there were still several squares to go on the chessboard. The king, realizing that he had been bamboozled by a crafty peasant, was nonetheless unwilling to admit that he had been wrong. He therefore ordered his royal baker to bake 100 loaves of bread, which he presented to the peasant with the claim that all of his requested grains of wheat were baked therein. The peasant, realizing that he had been counter-bamboozled by a crafty king, wisely took his bread and walked away while he still had a head on his shoulders.

Investigate

Follow these steps to find how much wheat would it actually have taken to fulfill the peasant's request.

1. Fill in the following table with the number of grains of wheat on each of the first 10 squares. The first three blanks are filled in for you.

Square	1	2	3	4	5	6	7	8	9	10	...
Number of Grains	1	2	4								...

2. Now fill in the following table with the running *total* of grains up to and including each of the first 10 squares. Again, the first three blanks are filled in for you.

Number of Squares	1	2	3	4	5	6	7	8	9	10	...
Total Number of Grains	1	3	7								...

3. Identify a relationship between the number of squares and the total number of grains. [*Hint*: Add one to each total and see if you can detect a pattern.]

4. Based on your answer to Exercise 3, write a formula for the total amount of wheat on all 64 squares. How many grains of wheat would it have taken to carry out the peasant's request?

It takes roughly 500 grains of wheat to fill a cubic inch. There are 2150 cubic inches in a bushel.

5. Convert the peasant's request to bushels of wheat.

6. In 1998, according to U.S. Department of Agriculture statistics, the total annual wheat production of the United States was 2,550,383,000 bushels. How many years would it take for the United States to produce enough wheat to satisfy the peasant's simple request?

Wheat on a Chessboard (continued)

• •

The reason this number is so big is because the number of grains grows *exponentially* as the number of chessboard squares increases. You can see this growth on your calculator by typing two commands on your home screen as shown in the screen at right. Then each time you press $\boxed{\text{ENTER}}$, you will see how the wheat mounts up—slowly at first, but eventually by huge steps. These commands may help you answer the following exercises.

```
0→A                    0
A+1→A:2^A-1
                       1
                       3
                       7
```

Exercises

1. Approximately how many grains of wheat are in a bushel?

2. How many squares of the chessboard are covered when the total amount of wheat first exceeds a bushel?

3. How many squares are covered when the total number of grains first exceeds a million?

4. How many grains of wheat does it take to cover the first row of the chessboard?

5. How many grains of wheat does it take to cover the top half of the chessboard?

6. How many squares of the chessboard could be covered to match the total 1998 U.S. wheat production?

7. **Challenge** The total land area of the United States is 3,536,488 square miles. How deep would the wheat on the 64-square chessboard be if it were evenly distributed over this entire area?

Manipulating a Polynomial   Activity 23

Consider the graph of the polynomial function $f(x) = 5x^4 - 17x^3 + 13x^2 - 8x + 12$ graphed in the ZDecimal viewing window:

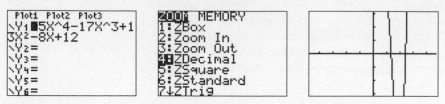

As you can see, this graph is not very informative, although it does show two real zeros of the polynomial. In this exploration you will learn how to set an appropriate viewing window. We will also use the Factor Theorem to add more real zeros (and hence more x-intercepts to the graph).

Investigate

1. Notice that there seems to be a turning point between $x = 1$ and $x = 3$. Go to **TRACE** and type in **2** and press **ENTER**. The calculator will show the y-coordinate at $x = 2$.

2. In order to capture that turning point on the screen, go to WINDOW and set Ymin $= -10$, leaving everything else the same. What happens to the x-axis in the graph?

3. In order to re-center the x-axis, set Ymax $= 10$. Notice that we can't quite see the y-intercept in the graph. Explain how the equation of the polynomial function confirms this result.

4. In order to capture the y-intercept with some room to spare, set Ymax $= 20$. Set Ymin to an appropriate value to keep the x-axis centered. The graph of $f(x)$ should now look pretty good although the y-axis has a 'fuzzy' appearance. Explain why this is so.

5. In order to turn off the tic marks on the y-axis, set Yscl $= 0$. Your graph should look like the graph at the right.

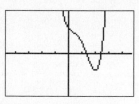

If the polynomial had more real zeros, you would want to see them on our screen as x-intercepts. The *Fundamental Theorem of Algebra* says that there could be at most two more real zeros, but in fact there are no more. Notice that the graph has a slight turn as it crosses the y-axis. If there were any more zeros, that turn would have bent down far enough to cross the x-axis, but in this graph it didn't. You can conclude that the other two zeros of this polynomial must be imaginary numbers.

Manipulating a Polynomial (continued)

Investigation

Suppose you would like to modify the graph to cross the x-axis at $x = -1$. This can easily be accomplished by multiplying the original polynomial by $(x + 1)$:

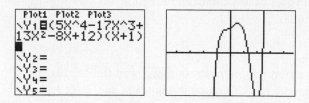

1. Explain why the Factor Theorem guarantees that the graph of this new polynomial will cross the x-axis at $x = -1$.

2. Adjust the window to bring all the turning points into view.

3. Put in another zero at $x = -3$.

4. Adjust the window to bring all turning points into view.

Exercises

1. Construct a polynomial with a graph that crosses the x-axis at $-3, 1, 3,$ and 5. Graph the polynomial in a window that shows all the x-intercepts and all the turning points.

2. Graph the polynomial $y = 2x^4 + 3x^3 + 5x^2 + 35$ in the ZDecimal window. Why is this window unsatisfactory?

3. Find an appropriate window to show the graph of the polynomial in Exercise 2.

Writing a Simple Program

Activity 24

In this exploration, you will learn how to write a simple program on your calculator. In fact, everything your calculator does relies on programs; the only difference here is that you will be writing it rather than the people who wrote the software for your calculator. The program you will write will find the roots of any quadratic function. As you should expect, it will rely on the quadratic formula.

Investigate

1. Press **PRGM** ▶ ▶ NEW to create a new program. Press **ENTER** and the calculator will ask you to name your new program. You can name it whatever you want (up to 8 characters). Here, the name QUADSOLV has been chosen so that its purpose can be more easily remembered. Press **ENTER** again to get the screen on the far right.

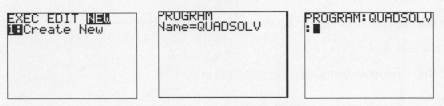

2. First, you will set the calculator modes. Press **MODE** to obtain a slightly different mode screen from what you are used to seeing. You want the calculator to show both real and imaginary solutions, so move down to the seventh line and choose 'a+bi'. It will show up on the first line of your program when you press **ENTER**.

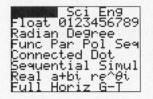 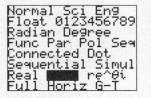 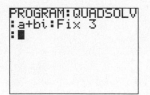

3. It helps to keep the displayed answers short enough to fit on the screen. The command 'Fix 3' will round answers to 3 decimal places. Put 'Fix 3' on the first line of the program by typing **ALPHA** [:] **MODE**. Use the arrow keys to position

   the cursor over the '3' in the second line and press **ENTER**. Then press **ENTER** again to move to the next line of the program.

4. The next step is to program the calculator to prompt the user for the coefficients of the quadratic expression $ax^2 + bx + c$. Press **PRGM** ▶ to access the I/O (Input/Output) commands. Select 'Prompt' by pressing **2**. The command 'Prompt' will appear on the next line of your program. Press **ALPHA** [A] **,** **ALPHA** [B] **,** **ALPHA** [C] to get the screen at right. When the program runs, the user will be prompted to input the values of A, B, and C.

Writing a Simple Program (continued)

5. On the next line insert the command 'Disp', found in the I/O submenu of `PRGM`. Complete the third line of the program by pressing `2nd` [A-LOCK] and entering the alpha characters. "ROOTS:". Press `ENTER` to go to the next line.

6. Choose 'Disp' again from the PRGM I/O menu and press `ENTER`. Carefully type in the quadratic formula for the first root as shown. Do not use quotes around it this time; this lets the calculator know that you want it to display the number, not the actual algebraic expression. Finish the line with the 'convert to fraction' symbol found in the `MATH` menu. Press `ENTER` to move to the next line. Repeat this process on the next line to display the second root.

First Root   Second Root

7. Finally, it is a good idea at the end of the program to set the modes back to what you are used to seeing. Repeat steps 2 and 3, but this time choose 'Real' and 'Float'.

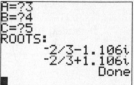

8. Press `2nd` [QUIT] to leave the programming screen and return to the home screen. To run the program, press `PRGM` again. In the EXEC (execute) menu, highlight QUADSOLV and press `ENTER`. The name of the program will appear on the screen. Press `ENTER` again and it will begin running. Enter a value for A, B, and C. The screen at right shows that the

roots of $y = 3x^2 + 4x + 5$ are $x = -\dfrac{2}{3} - 1.106i$ and $x = -\dfrac{2}{3} + 1.106i$.

Exercises

1. Enter values of A, B, and C that will give integer answers.

2. Enter values of A, B, and C that will give two roots that are the same.

3. Enter values of A, B, and C that will give pure imaginary answers.

4. Enter values of A, B, and C that will give rational real answers.

5. Enter values of A, B, and C that will give irrational real answers.

6. Challenge The formula $A = P\left(1 + \frac{r}{n}\right)^{nt}$ is used to calculate the value of an account after t years where P is the principle (initial deposit), r is the interest rate (expressed as a decimal), and n is the number of compounding periods per year. Write a program that prompts the user to input a value for $P, r, n,$ and t and then calculates the value of the account A.

a. Use your program to determine the account balance after 3 years for an initial deposit of $500, interest rate 7.5%, and monthly compounding.

b. Use your program to determine the account balance after 2 years and 3 months for an initial deposit of $2000, interest rate 5%, and quarterly compounding.

Repeated Radicals

Activity 25

What is the value of $2 + \sqrt{2 + \sqrt{2 + \sqrt{2 + \sqrt{2 + \ldots}}}}$? This is called a *repeated radical*, and the three dots indicate that the process of taking square roots and adding two is repeated infinitely. Infinite processes like these do not always obey the expected rules of algebra, since they do not always converge to real numbers. When they do converge, however, you can usually explore that convergence with a calculator.

Investigate

To find the value of the repeated radical above, start by entering **2** [ENTER] on the home screen. Then type the command **2** [+] [2nd] [√] [2nd] [ANS] [ )] and press [ENTER] again. Since the previous number on the screen (which the calculator calls 'Ans') was 2, the calculator shows the value of the expression

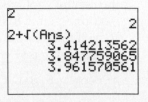

$2 + \sqrt{2}$. This becomes the new value of 'Ans', so pressing [ENTER] again will give the value of $2 + \sqrt{2 + \sqrt{2}}$. Repeatedly pressing [ENTER] will give the values of

$$2 + \sqrt{2 + \sqrt{2 + \sqrt{2}}},\ 2 + \sqrt{2 + \sqrt{2 + \sqrt{2 + \sqrt{2}}}},\ 2 + \sqrt{2 + \sqrt{2 + \sqrt{2 + \sqrt{2 + \sqrt{2}}}}}\ldots.$$

The numbers on your screen are approaching the value of the repeated radical, 4. In fact, they will soon get so close to 4 that the calculator will not be able to tell the difference. From that point on, $2 + \sqrt{\ }$ (Ans) will be interpreted as $2 + \sqrt{4}$ every time, which is exactly 4. This investigation suggests that

$$2 + \sqrt{2 + \sqrt{2 + \sqrt{2 + \sqrt{2 + \ldots}}}} = 4.$$

It is also possible to find the value of a repeated radical by solving a quadratic equation.

$$x = 2 + \sqrt{2 + \sqrt{2 + \sqrt{2 + \sqrt{2 + \ldots}}}}$$ Let x equal the repeated radical expression.

$$x - 2 = \sqrt{2 + \sqrt{2 + \sqrt{2 + \sqrt{2 + \ldots}}}}$$ Subtract 2.

$$(x - 2)^2 = \left(\sqrt{2 + \sqrt{2 + \sqrt{2 + \sqrt{2 + \ldots}}}} \right)^2$$ Square both sides.

$$x^2 - 4x + 4 = 2 + \sqrt{2 + \sqrt{2 + \sqrt{2 + \ldots}}}$$ Expand.

$x^2 - 4x + 4 = x$ Right side is equal to x.

$x^2 - 5x + 4 = 0$ Subtract x.

$(x - 4)(x - 1) = 0$ Factor.

$x - 4 = 0$ or $x - 1 = 0$ Zero-Factor Property

$x = 4$ or $x = 1$

Reject the extraneous root $x = 1$, since the repeated radical is obviously bigger than 2. That leaves the solution $x = 4$, which is what the calculator implied in the first place. Keep in mind that the calculator *suggested* the value of the repeated radical, whereas the algebraic computation *proved* that it is equal to 4.

Repeated Radicals (continued)

Exercises

1. Adapt the calculator steps given in the investigation to discover the value of
$$6 + \sqrt{6 + \sqrt{6 + \sqrt{6 + \sqrt{6 + \ldots}}}}\,.$$

2. Prove that your value is correct by solving an appropriate quadratic equation.

3. Use your calculator to discover the value of $3 + \sqrt{3 + \sqrt{3 + \sqrt{3 + \sqrt{3 + \ldots}}}}$.
   Do you recognize this number? Do you suppose it is the exact value?

4. Use the quadratic formula to find the *exact* value of
   $3 + \sqrt{3 + \sqrt{3 + \sqrt{3 + \sqrt{3 + \ldots}}}}$. Is this number rational or irrational? Enter
   the exact value on your calculator to confirm that it matches the approximation
   found in Exercise 3.

5. What do the answers to the preceding two Exercises suggest about the need for
   algebra in a calculator age?

Asymptotes and Holes

Activity 26

Unlike with polynomial functions, rational functions have denominators that may possibly take on the value zero. Since division by zero is impossible, such values cannot be in the domain of the rational function. What happens to the graph at such values (called *singularities*) is quite interesting, and not always the same. The investigation given below will illustrate what can happen.

Investigate

1. Graph the function $y = \dfrac{2}{x^2 - 4}$ in the ZDecimal viewing window as Y1. Where does the function appear to be undefined? Does this make sense algebraically?

2. Press TRACE and use the arrow keys to move the cursor until you land on each of the two singularities. What happens to the value of Y at these points?

3. What is happening to the function on either side of the singularities? Does this make sense algebraically? Try to explain why it does in words. If you are able to do this, you will have a good working definition of what it means for a function to have *asymptotes*.

4. Now graph the same function in the viewing window $-5 \le x \le 5$ and $-3 \le y \le 3$. Describe what happens to the graph.

5. It appears as if the calculator puts those extra lines there deliberately in order to show the asymptotes, but it doesn't. Press TRACE again and try to land on the singularity. Explain what happens (*Hint:* Look for a sign change in y.).

6. The calculator graph is made up of the very same values that you see when you trace along the curve. When it calculates the ordered pair shown at the bottom of the screen, it turns on the nearest pixel (the little dot on the screen). In 'Connected' mode, the calculator draws a line that connects consecutive points. Graph the function in 'Dot' mode (press MODE, place the cursor on DOT, and press ENTER) and notice the difference. Now explain where those extra lines came from in Exercise 4.

7. Place the calculator back in 'Connected' mode and graph the function $y = \dfrac{2x + 4}{x^2 - 4}$ in the ZDecimal viewing window. Do you still see a singularity at $x = 2$? Explain the appearance of the singularity at $x = -2$. (Look carefully!)

8. Press TRACE and verify that the function is still undefined at the same places. Explain why this makes sense algebraically.

9. Describe the difference in the behavior of the graph at the two singularities.

10. Use factoring to *simplify* the rational function in Exercise 7 and enter the simplified function as Y2. Turn off Y1 by moving the cursor to the '=' symbol and pressing ENTER. Now press GRAPH to view Y2. Do you get the same graph? Explain.

11. For an interesting demonstration of what happens at $x = -2$, go to the Y= screen and change the graphing style for both functions. Move the cursor to the left of Y1 (over the '\' symbol) and press ENTER four times to get the '–0' symbol. Also, make sure you turn on Y1 by positioning the cursor over '=' and pressing ENTER. Do the same for Y2, then press GRAPH and watch the graphing ball very carefully. Describe what you notice.

Asymptotes and Holes (continued)

If you have done this exploration from start to finish, you should now be able to tell the difference between an asymptote and a hole in the graph.

Exercises

1. The function $y = \dfrac{x^2 - 1}{x - 1}$ simplifies to $y = x + 1$. What is the difference between the graphs of the two functions? What is the domain of each function?

2. Construct a rational function with asymptotes at $x = 1$ and $x = -1$.

3. Construct a function with a graph that looks like the one at right.

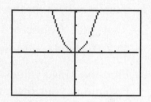

Extension

4. Another way to eliminate the false asymptotes on a graph screen is to change the value of ΔX (the step that the calculator takes from pixel to pixel along the x-axis).

   Graph the function $y = \dfrac{2}{x^2 - 4}$ in the window $-5 \le x \le 5$ and $-3 \le y \le 3$.

   Now type the command '.1 → ΔX' on the home screen and graph the function again (You'll find ΔX variable by pressing [VARS] [ENTER] **8 : ΔX.**). The reason this works is that the calculator will evaluate the function for all values of x where x is $-5, -4.9, \ldots, -2.1, -2, -1.9, \ldots, 1.9, 2, 2.1, \ldots 4.9, 5$. Notice that the calculator *will* evaluate the rational function at the singularities rather than skip over them.

5. Graph the rational function $y = \dfrac{1}{(1 - 2.05)(x - .95)}$ in the window $0 \le x \le 3$

   and $-10 \le y \le 10$. On the home screen, use the [STO▶] command with an appropriate value of ΔX to eliminate the false asymptotes on the graph.

Stepping Out

Activity 27

Most of the functions you study in algebra are *continuous*, which means (loosely) they have graphs you can draw without taking your pencil off the paper. One type of non-continuous function is called a *step function*. Your calculator happens to have a built-in step function called the *greatest integer function*, abbreviated as 'int', and defined as follows:

$$\text{int}(x) = \text{greatest integer less than or equal to } x.$$

Investigate

1. You'll find 'int' in the NUM submenu of the MATH menu. Put your calculator in 'Dot' (not 'Connected') mode and graph $y = \text{int}(x)$ in the ZDecimal (ZOOM **4 : ZDecimal**) window. Explain why $y = \text{int}(x)$ is called a step function.

2. Find the range values that correspond to the domain values $\{1.5, 2, \frac{34}{7}, \pi, 4.9999\}$. Explain in your own words what 'int' does to a number.

3. Find the range values that go with the domain values $\{-1.5, -2, -\frac{34}{7}, -\pi, -4.9999\}$. If necessary, refine your description of the function 'int'.

4. Why is it necessary to be in 'Dot' mode when graphing this function?

5. Each of the following graphs was produced in the Zdecimal window by making a slight modification to the function $y = \text{int}(x)$. For example, the first screen shows the graph of $y = \text{int}(2x)$. Try to produce the graphs in the other screens.

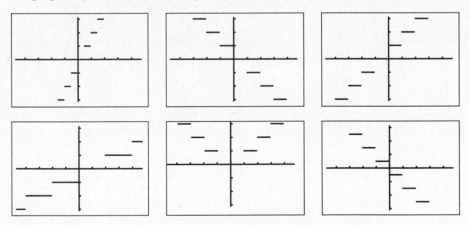

One example of a real-world step function is a taxicab fare function.

6. Suppose the Mellow Cab Company charges \$3.50 plus \$2.50 for each mile (or fraction thereof). Determine the cost of a $\frac{1}{2}$ mile trip and a $2\frac{1}{2}$ mile trip. Explain why the cost function $C(x) = 3.50 + 2.50x$ does not successfully model these costs.

7. The function $C(x) = 3.50 + 2.50 \, \text{int}(x)$ is better, but still not quite correct. Graph the function in an appropriate window and use TRACE to explain what is wrong.

8. Make a slight modification to the cost function, $C(x)$, to get the correct step function. (Your function should work for all values of x except integers. Don't worry about this slight inconsistency now.)

Stepping Out (continued)

Exercises

1. The cost to mail a first-class letter at the time this booklet was written was 34¢ for the first ounce and 23¢ for each additional ounce or fraction thereof, up to 13 ounces. Write a step function that will model the cost for $0 < x \leq 13$. (Don't worry about what happens with the integer domain values.)

2. The graphs of $y = \text{int}(x + 1)$ and $y = -\text{int}(-x)$ seem to show the same function, but they are subtly different. Use ⟨TRACE⟩ in the Zdecimal window to help explain what the difference is.

3. **Challenge** Go back to your answers to Exercise 8 in the investigation and Exercise 1 in the exercises and see if you can adapt the functions one more time so that they work correctly at the integer domain values.

Systems With Many Solutions

Activity 28

Having learned how to solve systems of equations on her calculator by $[A]^{-1}[B]$, Mavis, an aspiring math student and part-time fast-food cashier, was eager to practice at work. She noted that one customer bought 2 burgers, 3 fries, and 1 soft drink for $6.85. The next customer bought 4 burgers, 3 fries, and 3 soft drinks for $11.65. A third customer bought 3 burgers, 3 fries, and 2 soft drinks for $9.25. That made for three linear equations in three unknowns, just like at school. During her break, she put the matrices into her calculator and entered $[A]^{-1}[B]$, confident that she would get the store's prices for a burger, an order of fries, and a soft drink. Here's what happened.

Investigate

1. Enter the coefficients as matrix A and the total costs as matrix B. What happens when you evaluate $[A]^{-1}[B]$ on a calculator?

2. Mavis knew full well that her store charged $1.75 for a burger, $.90 for fries, and $.65 for a soft drink. Enter those values as matrix C and form the product $[A][C]$. Do you get the totals in matrix $[B]$?

3. Write out the three equations in three unknowns represented by Mavis's data. Does the system have a solution? Explain. (*Hint*: Now that you know what the store charges, do those numbers solve the system?)

4. If the system has a solution, why didn't the calculator find it?

When the calculator tries to find a solution using $[A]^{-1}[B]$, it is looking for a *unique* solution. The error message 'singular matrix' does not always mean that there is *no* solution; it might also mean that there are *many* solutions. Unfortunately for Mavis, that is what happened.

5. Suppose Mavis's store charged $2.05 for a burger, $.80 for an order of fries, and $.35 for a soft drink. What would the three customers have paid for their orders?

6. Suppose Mavis's store charged $1.45 for a burger, $1.00 for fries, and $.95 for a soft drink. What would the three customers have paid?

7. Explain why multiple answers prevent the $[A]^{-1}[B]$ method from working.

Exercises

1. As you might expect, the calculator can solve the system above, but you need to do it a different way. Use the 'Augment' command from the MATRIX MATH submenu to form a single matrix from A and B as shown below. Then select 'rref' from the same menu to get the augmented matrix into reduced row- echelon form. Finally, use the 'convert to fraction' command to get the matrix into more readable form.

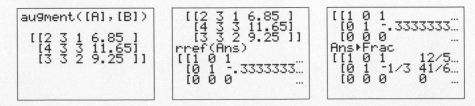

Systems With Many Solutions (continued)

2. The calculator has converted the original problem to an equivalent problem that looks like this:

$$\begin{bmatrix} 1 & 0 & 1 & 12/5 \\ 0 & 1 & -1/3 & 41/60 \\ 0 & 0 & 0 & 0 \end{bmatrix}.$$

The bottom row represents the equation $0x + 0y + 0z = 0$. Explain why this gives no information whatsoever about $x, y,$ and z.

3. The middle row represents the equation $y - \dfrac{1}{3}z = \dfrac{41}{60}$. Show that this is equivalent to the equation $3y - z = 2.05$.

4. What equation is represented by the top row?

5. Since the bottom row gives no information, any solution to the top two rows will solve the entire system. Let $y = \$.75$ be the price of an order of fries. Use the equations from Exercises 3 and 4 to find the corresponding values of x and z.

6. Show that your prices found in question 5 satisfy Mavis's original three equations.

Extend

The equations that result from the top two rows of the augmented matrix both contain the variable z. You can eliminate the variable z and obtain a third equation in just x and y. If you solve this equation for y, it can be entered as Y1 on a graphing calculator as seen below. Y2 represents the first equation, $2x + 3y + z = 6.85$, written in terms of X and Y1. The screens below show how the table feature can be used to see a list of solutions to the original system.

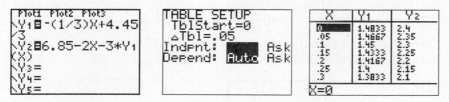

7. The third screen above gives the costs of a burger (X), fries (Y1), and a soft drink (Y2). Give two reasons why the values shown in the screens above are not reasonable.

8. Go to **2nd** [TBLSET] and change 'TlbStart' to a value that is more reasonable. Scroll through the table and find three different sets of values that seem reasonable.

Parabolic Reflectors

Activity 29

You might not expect to run into parabolas outside of your algebra classroom, but you can see them everywhere once you know where to look. A 40-yard touchdown pass follows a parabolic path from the quarterback to the wide receiver. If you watch the pass on television, you are probably seeing a signal that was sent from a parabolic transmitter, bounced off a satellite, and picked up by a parabolic receiver back on Earth. Drive by a television station sometime and notice all the parabolic dishes aimed at the sky—each one designed to gather signal waves from a particular source and focus them to a single point so that they can then be beamed on to you. That "focusing" property of parabolas is the secret behind satellite dishes, flashlights, automobile headlamps, large telescopes, and dozens of other useful devices. Here is an exploration to give you new respect for parabolas and what they can do.

Investigate

1. In the **2nd** [FORMAT] menu, place the cursor on 'AxesOff' to turn off the *x*-axis and *y*-axis temporarily. (When you are done with this exploration, remember to go back and choose 'AxesOn'.)

2. In the WINDOW shown below, graph the parabola $y = .25x^2$.

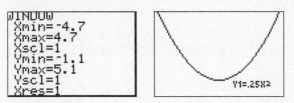

3. The *focus* of the parabola $y = ax^2$ is a special point $4a$ units above the vertex. In this case, the focus is the point $(0, 1)$. To turn this point on from the home screen, go to the **2nd** [DRAW] menu, choose the POINTS submenu, and select the Pt-On command. Finish it as 'Pt-On(0,1,2)' and press **ENTER** to turn on the point $(0, 1)$ with the little square mark, which the calculator considers mark #2.

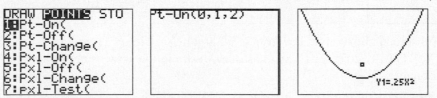

4. Thanks to the shape of the parabola, every ray that strikes the parabola and is parallel to the axis of symmetry will be reflected directly to the focus. That's how the satellite dish works. Conversely, every ray that emanates from the focus will be reflected parallel to the axis of symmetry. That's how a flashlight works. To see why this is believable, we can draw some rays. On the home screen, type '3 **STO►** **ALPHA** [A] **ENTER**' to let A = 3. Then type (carefully) the 'Line' command (which you'll find in the DRAW menu) exactly as shown on the screen below. When you press **ENTER**, you will see the rays.

Parabolic Reflectors (continued)

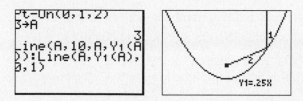

The angle of incidence (marked with a '1' on the diagram above) is defined as the angle between the incoming ray and the parabola. The angle of reflection (marked with a '2' on the diagram above) is the angle formed by the reflected ray and the parabola.

5. What appears to be true about the angle of incidence and the angle of reflection?

6. To draw more rays, go back to the home screen and store a new value for A, making sure that $-4.7 \leq A \leq 4.7$. Then press **2nd** **ENTER** **2nd** **ENTER** to get the 'Line' command back. When you see it on the screen, press **ENTER** . It will draw the new rays. Do this as many times as you wish; the parabola never gets tired!

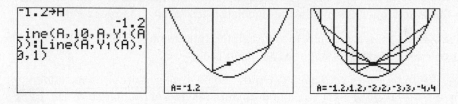

Exercises

1. What point is the focus of the parabola $y = x^2$?

2. As a parabola gets shallower, does the focus move closer to the vertex or farther away?

3. Before electricity, lighthouses had to rely on the light from oil lamps to warn ships. Explain how a parabolic mirror could make this possible.

Algebra 2 Activity 29   **63**

Exploring Powers of –1   Activity 30

You have learned enough about exponents and real numbers to know that $(-1)^2 = 1$, $(-1)^3 = -1$, $(-1)^{\frac{1}{3}} = -1$, and $(-1)^{\frac{1}{2}}$ is undefined. On a little more complicated level, $(-1)^{\frac{2}{3}} = 1$, and $(-1)^{\frac{3}{2}}$ is undefined. On a much more subtle level, $(-1)^{\frac{4}{6}} = 1$, $(-1)^{\frac{2}{6}} = -1$, and $(-1)^{\frac{6}{8}}$ is undefined. This makes the function $y = (-1)^x$ a very interesting function to graph.

Investigate

1. On the home screen, verify the powers of -1 mentioned in the preceding paragraph.

2. Use the calculator to compare $(-1)^{\frac{2}{6}}$ to $((-1)^2)^{\frac{1}{6}}$. Is this result consistent with the laws of exponents?

3. Based on your results from the previous exercise, explain how your calculator evaluates $(-1)^{\frac{2}{6}}$.

4. Enter the function $y = (-1)^x$ as Y1 and graph it in the ZDecimal window. `TRACE` along the graph and explain how the calculator determines the range values.

5. Change Xmin to $-\pi$ and Xmax to π. Graph the function again. Can you explain the graph you see? [It might help to `TRACE` again.]

6. Change Xmin to -8 and Xmax to 8. On the home screen, store .2 as the increment in x by typing '.2 `STO▶` Δx' (You'll find Δx in the [Window] submenu of the `VARS` menu.). Graph the function again. Describe the graph.

7. Now change Xmin to -20, Xmax to 20, and XScl to 5. Store .4 as Δx. Graph the function again. Explain what happens this time.

8. Finally, change Xmin to -19, Xmax to 19, and store .4 as Δx again. (You will have to store it again, after changing Xmin and Xmax.) Graph the function again. Explain what happens this time.

You might think that all of this strange behavior would disqualify $y = (-1)^x$ from the world of respectable functions, and you would be right. That is why most books (including ours) are careful to restrict the definition of *exponential functions* to functions of the form $y = a^x$ for $a > 0$ (and $a \neq 1$). On the other hand, your calculator knows that the laws of exponents allow *some* powers of negative numbers to be defined consistently, namely those of the form $a^{m/n}$ with n odd and m/n in lowest terms. It handles those powers as special cases, and those are the only powers that show up on the graphs!

Exercises

1. Change the base of the function in Y1 to produce each of the following graphs in the Zdecimal window:

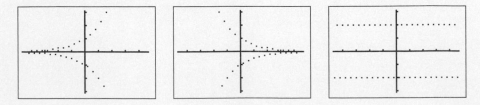

Exploring Powers of –1 (continued)

2. If x is equal to $\dfrac{m}{n}$, a quotient of integers in lowest terms, then we can rewrite the function in radical notation using the definition $a^x = a^{m/n} = \sqrt[n]{a^m}$. Explain why this definition does not define 2^π. How could you use the definition to get a good approximation of 2^π if you need one?

Bull's-eyes

Activity 31

All lines of the form $y = 2x + k$ are parallel to each other, since they all have slope 2. Similarly, all lines of the form $y = kx + 2$ go through the y-axis at 2, since they all have the same y-intercept. These are called *families of functions*, and their graphs usually show interesting patterns. Shown below are representative members of the two families of lines we have just described. (You should be able to spot which family is which.)

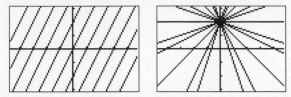

In this activity, you will create "bull's-eye" patterns using families of functions generated with a list of numbers.

Investigate

1. First, store the numbers 1 through 6 in **L1** by typing {1,2,3,4,5,6} STO▶ 2nd [L1] on the home screen and pressing ENTER .

2. For the classic bull's-eye, type the functions in Y1 and Y2 exactly as shown (Y1 can be found by pressing VARS ▶ [Y-VARS] ENTER ENTER). Graph the family in the Zdecimal window.

3. You will now keep the window and Y2 the same and make subtle changes to Y1. The classic bull's-eye, obviously, is made up of circles. Try each of these and see if you can identify the shapes.

4. Which of the bull's-eyes above are made up of pieces of parabolas?

5. Notice that only a slight change is made from the first screen in Exercise 3 to the second screen. Make another slight change to the first screen to produce the bull's-eye shown in screen at right.

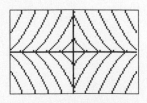

Bull's-eyes (continued)

Exercises

1. Find the domain and range of each of the Y1 functions in the investigation above when **L1** takes on the value 4.

2. Graph the bull's-eye determined when $Y_1 = \left(\sqrt{L1} - \sqrt{|x|}\right)^2$ and $Y_2 = -Y_1$. (This is called a hypocycloid.)

3. Create a different bull's-eye pattern of your own.

The Natural Logarithm

Activity 32

The *natural logarithm* function is defined to be the logarithm function with base e, where e is an irrational number a little bigger than 2.7. You can get a 10-digit approximation of e on your calculator by pressing the e button (**2nd** [e]) on your calculator.

```
e
              2.718281828
```

A logical question that occurs to most algebra students is, "What is so natural about that?" It is hard to find a good answer to that question by looking at history, since the first logarithms were tables of numbers derived without a concept of "base" at all, let alone a concept of e. It was only after mathematicians learned more about logarithmic functions that it became evident that natural logarithms had many interesting applications. By that time, the man generally credited for inventing them, John Napier, had been dead for about sixty years.

Investigate

1. In the window shown below, graph the function $y = \dfrac{1}{x}$.

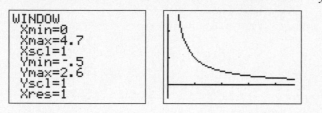

2. On the home screen, type the two 'Line' commands (located in the **2nd** [DRAW] menu) as shown, connected by a colon, and press **ENTER** . You will get a square drawn on the graph. What is the area of this square?

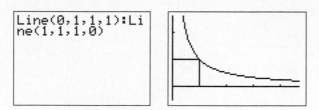

3. How far to the right of $x = 1$ do we need to go so that the area under the curve from $x = 1$ to that point is the same as the area of the square? There is an "area finder" in the **2nd** [CALC] menu that will enable us to check this out. Press **2nd** [CALC] **7 : ∫f(x)dx.** The calculator will ask you for a lower limit, and you should press **1** **ENTER** . (This response will remain the same throughout this exploration.) The calculator will then ask for an upper limit. It looks like we need to go somewhere between 2 and 3, so choose **2** **·** **5** **ENTER** . The calculator will shade in the area and then announce what it equals.

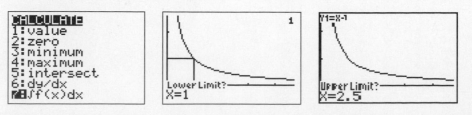

The Natural Logarithm (continued)

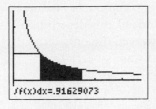

∫f(x)dx=.91629073

4. As you can see, the area is not quite the same as the area of the square. Erase this attempt by typing **2nd** [DRAW] **1 : ClrDraw.** This will unfortunately erase the square also, but you can get it back by returning to the home screen and pressing **2nd** **ENTER** to redo the Line command. Now experiment with the upper limit until you find the number that makes the area exactly equal to the area of the square. Do you recognize the number?

Exercises

1. Use $\int f(x)dx$ as in the investigation above to find the area under the graph of $y = \dfrac{1}{x}$ between $x = 1$ and $x = 2$. Return to the home screen and type **2nd** [ANS] **ENTER** to display the area on the home screen. Beneath it, type **LN** **2** **)** **ENTER** . What do you notice about the two numbers?

2. Press **2nd** [DRAW] **1 : ClrDraw** to clear the drawing. Choose a random number a between 1 and 4.7 and repeat the steps of Exercise 1 using a as the upper limit. What do you notice about the area and ln a?

3. Clear the drawing again. Choose a random number a between 0 and 1 (non-inclusive) and repeat the steps of Exercise 1 using a as the upper limit. (Don't worry that the upper limit is less than the lower limit; the calculator will handle it.) What do you notice about the area and ln a?

4. What happens to the area reported by the calculator when the upper limit is less than the lower limit?

5. Using the results from this exploration, construct a "natural" definition of ln(a) based on the area under the graph of $y = \dfrac{1}{x}$.

Can a Graph Cross Its Own Asymptote?   Activity 33

Intuitively, an asymptote can be thought of as a line that a graph *approaches* to an arbitrary degree of closeness but does not actually *intersect*. Indeed, this description is often perfectly accurate. In the definition of an asymptote, however, the only thing that matters is the closeness condition. Non-intersection is not really an issue, as this exploration will show.

Investigate

1. Enter the functions $Y1 = \dfrac{1}{(x + 1)}$ and $Y2 = \dfrac{x}{(x^2 + 1)}$
   and graph them in the window shown. Find the
   horizontal asymptote of each function.

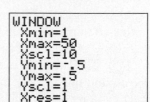

```
WINDOW
 Xmin=1
 Xmax=50
 Xscl=10
 Ymin=-.5
 Ymax=.5
 Yscl=1
 Xres=1
```

2. Will the graph of either function intersect the asymptote
   as x approaches infinity?

3. Now graph the same two functions in the ZDecimal
   window. Does either graph intersect its own asymptote?

4. Graph the function $y = \dfrac{3(x^2 - 1)}{x^4}$ in the ZDecimal window. How many times does
   this graph cross its own asymptote?

5. Repeat Exercise 4 using the function $y = \dfrac{5(x^3 - x)}{x^6 + 1}$. How many times does this
   graph cross its own asymptote?

6. Do you think a graph could cross its own asymptote fifty times?

Exercises

1. Construct a rational function that crosses its asymptote four times: at $x = \pm 1$ and
   $x = \pm 2$.

2. The function $y = \dfrac{\sin(x)}{x}$ is something of a phenomenon in the world of functions
   that cross their own asymptotes. Graph the function in the original window and
   explain what is meant by this.

3. Is the line $y = 2$ an asymptote for the graph of the function $y = 2$? Explain.

4. Surprisingly, a graph can even intersect its own *vertical* asymptote. Fill in the blanks
   below to define a split function with a vertical asymptote at $x = 0$ that is
   intersected by the graph.
   $$f(x) = \begin{cases} \frac{1}{x} \text{ if } x > 0 \\ \underline{\quad} \text{ if } \underline{\quad} \end{cases}.$$

Making Ellipses out of Circles   Activity 34

The 'Y=' editor on your calculator allows you to graph relations that are functions. An ellipse, which clearly fails the vertical line test, is not a function and therefore cannot be directly graphed using the 'Y=' editor. You have probably seen one fix for this problem, which is to graph the upper and lower halves of the ellipse as separate functions. For example, one way to produce a graph of the horizontal ellipse centered at (0, 0) with a major axis of length 6 and a minor axis of length 4 is to write the equation of the ellipse in standard form and solve it for *y:*

$$\frac{x^2}{9} + \frac{y^2}{4} = 1 \rightarrow y = \pm\sqrt{4 - \frac{4x^2}{9}}$$

Now the ellipse can be graphed in the 'Y=' editor as shown below.

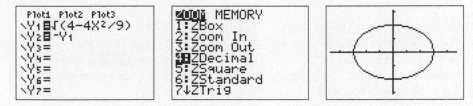

The purpose of this exploration is to give you another way of graphing an ellipse, using the fact that an ellipse is just a circle that has been stretched horizontally and vertically by different factors.

Investigate

1. Clear all functions from the [Y=] screen. Select ZDecimal from the [WINDOW] screen to set up a *square* window. On the home screen, choose the 'Circle(' command from the [2nd] [DRAW] menu and type the command shown below. When you press [ENTER], the calculator will produce a graph of a circle with center $(0, 0)$ and radius 1.

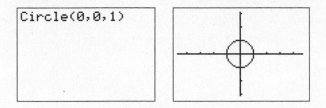

2. Now you will change the window. Go to the [WINDOW] screen, set your cursor at the end of the first line, and type [÷] 3 [ENTER] to divide Xmin by 3. Do the same for Xmax and Xscl.

3. Continuing, type [÷] 2 [ENTER] at the end of the next line to divide Ymin by 2. Do the same for Ymax and Yscl. Your final window will look like the screen at right.

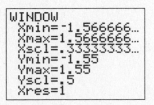

4. Return to the home screen and press [2nd] [ENTER] to draw that same circle again. Explain what happens to the graph.

5. Explain in your own words how this method works.

Making Ellipses out of Circles (continued)

Exercises

1. Use the method described in the investigation to draw a vertical ellipse with major axis of length 6 and minor axis of length 4. This will produce the same ellipse drawn in the investigation, rotated 90°.

2. Draw a horizontal ellipse with a major axis of length 8 and a minor axis of length 6.

3. Explain how you can draw a horizontal ellipse with a major axis of length 12 and a minor axis of length 4. Graph the ellipse.

Extend

4. As you probably discovered in Exercise 3, the ellipse goes off the screen if it is graphed in the ZDecimal window. You can fix this by taking an extra step to enlarge the window. After modifying the ZDecimal screen, go to WINDOW and multiply Xmin, Xmax, Ymin, and Ymax by 2. This will give you a square window that is twice as big. Redo Exercise 3 using this larger window.

5. Use the technique described in 4 to graph a vertical ellipse with a major axis of length 12 and a minor axis of length 6.

6. **Challenge** Draw the ellipse described in 5, with center at (2, 3). (*Hint*: Graph the ellipse centered at the origin and use TRACE to determine where the coordinates of the center should be located.)

The Harmonic Series

Activity 35

You have learned that some infinite series have finite sums. For example, the infinite geometric series $\frac{1}{2} + \frac{1}{4} + \frac{1}{8} + \cdots + \frac{1}{2^n} + \cdots$ converges to a sum of 1. On the other hand, some infinite series simply grow without bound, like $1 + 2 + 3 + 4 + \cdots + n + \cdots$. Since it is bad mathematical practice to say that such a series "adds up to infinity," we say that the series "diverges to infinity," or simply "diverges."

Easily, one of the more interesting divergent series is the *harmonic series*, which is defined as $1 + \frac{1}{2} + \frac{1}{3} + \frac{1}{4} + \cdots + \frac{1}{n} + \cdots$.

The terms get so small in the long run that it is easy to believe the series must converge to a finite sum. This exploration might help to convince you that it does not, while also giving you an idea of how it diverges at such an excruciatingly slow rate.

Investigate

If you have already done the activity titled *The Natural Logarithm*, you would have learned that the first-quadrant area under the graph of the function $y = \frac{1}{x}$ between $x = 1$ and $x = a$ is exactly equal to ln a. In the examples given below, the area under $y = \frac{1}{x}$ between $x = 1$ and $x = 3$ is equal to $\ln(3) \approx 1.099$. Likewise, the area between $x = 1$ and $x = 5.2$ is equal to $\ln(5.2) \approx 1.649$.

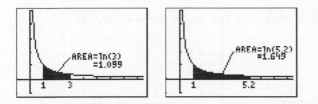

1. The next step is to explore what happens to this area as a goes off toward infinity. Equivalently, we can ask what happens to $\ln(a)$ as a goes off toward infinity. Below is the graph of $y = \ln(x)$:

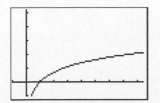

Does this graph keep rising without bound? Is it bounded above, perhaps by a horizontal asymptote?

2. If you were not sure of the answer to Exercise 1, remember that the range of $y = \ln(x)$ is the same as the domain of its inverse function. What is the inverse function, and what is its domain?

This situation can also be analyzed by looking at areas related to $y = \frac{1}{x}$.

Algebra 2 Activity 35   **73**

The Harmonic Series (continued)

3. In the pictures below, what are the areas of the rectangles shown?

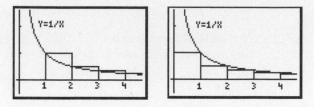

4. Use the screen on the left above to explain why $1 + \dfrac{1}{2} + \dfrac{1}{3} + \cdots + \dfrac{1}{a} > \ln(a)$.

   Use the screen on the right to explain why $1 + \dfrac{1}{2} + \dfrac{1}{3} + \cdots + \dfrac{1}{a} < 1 + \ln(a)$.

5. According to Exercise 4, the sum of the first 10,000 terms of the harmonic series,
   $1 + \dfrac{1}{2} + \dfrac{1}{3} + \dfrac{1}{4} + \cdots + \dfrac{1}{10,000}$, will be a number between $\ln(10,000)$ and
   $1 + \ln(10,000)$. About how big is this sum?

Exercises

1. The 'seq' command is located in the OPS submenu of the **2nd** [LIST] menu.
   To build the first 100 terms of the harmonic sequence, type the command on the
   screen below and press **ENTER** . (The 'convert to fraction' command at the end of the
   line is in the **MATH** menu.)

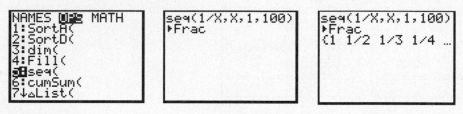

2. To sum the terms, choose 'sum' in the MATH submenu of the **2nd** [LIST] menu,
   finishing the command with **2nd** [ANS]. What is the sum of the first 100 terms of
   the harmonic series? Show that it lies between $\ln(100)$ and $1 + \ln(100)$.

3. The single command 'sum(seq(1/X,X,1,500))' will sum the first 500 terms of
   the harmonic series. Find the sum and verify that it lies between $\ln(500)$ and
   $1 + \ln(500)$.

4. Does the sum of the first billion terms of the harmonic series get bigger than 25?
   (*Note:* Don't try to use the 'sum(' and 'seq(' commands!)

5. About how many terms of the harmonic series would you need to add up in order
   to get a sum of 100? (*Hint:* Use the inverse function of $\ln(x)$).

Monte Carlo Pi

Activity 36

Computers enable mathematicians to answer questions of many different kinds by setting up models and running computer simulations. When the simulations involve probability, the computer method of solution is often called the *Monte Carlo Method*. In this exploration, we will use the Monte Carlo method to approximate the value of π.

Investigate

1. The graph at right shows a unit square in the first quadrant. The shaded region is a quarter of the interior of the unit circle. If a point is chosen at random inside the square, what is the probability it lies inside the shaded area?

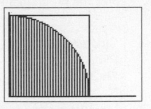

2. Set the window as shown below. On the home screen, execute the three commands shown (all located in the **2nd** [DRAW] menu). You should get the screen on the right.

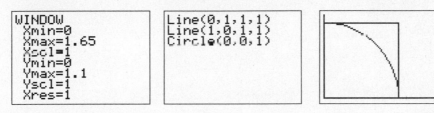

3. Return to the home screen. Clear the previous commands by pressing **CLEAR** and type in the command shown below. 'Rand' is located in the PRB submenu of the **MATH** menu. It gives a random number between 0 and 1. The 'Pt-On' command is in the POINTS submenu of the **2nd** [DRAW] menu. When you press **ENTER**, the point (A,B) will be turned on in the picture. Why must it lie inside the square?

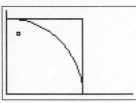

4. Quit to the home screen and press **ENTER** again. The calculator will turn on another point. Keep doing this until you have found a total of 20 points. Calculate the ratio of the number of those points that lie inside the circle to the total number of points created. Multiply the ratio by 4. Compare the result to π.

5. The *Law of Large Numbers* predicts that the result of your calculations in Exercise 4 will get closer to π as the number of points gets larger. Find the class average of the result calculated in Exercise 4 to get a large number of points. Compare the result to π.

Monte Carlo Pi (continued)

Exercises

1. A good way to get a large number of points without much effort is to write a short
   program. The program shown below will input the number of points from the user
   and will announce the eventual approximation of π. Explain what each line of the
   program does. (See the exploration *Writing a Simple Program* for help on how to
   enter the program into your calculator.)

```
ClrDraw
PlotsOff
FnOff
0→Xmin:1.6→Xmax:1→Xscl:0→Ymin:1.1→Ymax:1→Yscl
Line(0,1,1,1) :Line(1,0,1,1) :Circle(0,0,1)
0→H
Input "HOW MANY POINTS?" ,N
For(K,1,N)
rand →A:rand →B
Pt-On(A,B,1)
If A² + B² ≤ 1
H+1→H
End
Disp "4*RATIO IS:"
Disp 4H/N
```

2. Enter the program into your calculator with the name "MCPI" and run the
   simulation with N = 100. Merge the results with those of your classmates.
   How close is your Monte Carlo approximation to the true value of π?

The Way the Ball Bounces

Activity 37

One of the reasons we study trigonometric functions on the unit circle is to appreciate the connection between trigonometry and *harmonic motion*. A good example of harmonic motion is the bouncing of a ball attached to the bottom of a spring. When the ball is pulled down, the spring stretches. When the ball is released, it begins bouncing up and down, at first pulled up by the spring, then pulled back down by gravity, then pulled back up by the spring, and so forth. In this investigation we will see what this has to do with trigonometry and the unit circle.

Investigate

1. First, graph the unit circle trigonometrically, using the fact that every point on the unit circle is of the form $(\cos(T), \sin(T))$ for some angle T. Press **MODE** and put your

   graphing calculator in parametric ('Par') and Radian mode. In the **Y=** screen, enter $X_{1T} = \cos(T)$ and $Y_{1T} = \sin(T)$. Set the **WINDOW** as shown below (note that Tmax $= 2\pi$), and press **GRAPH** to get the unit circle.

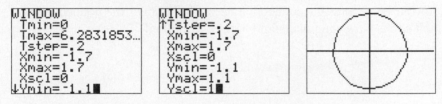

2. Next, you set a ball in motion around the unit circle. Change Tmax to 6π (so it will go around three times) and go to the **Y=** screen. Move the cursor to the left of X_{1T} and press **ENTER** three times to change the graph style from '\' to '0' (the moving ball). When you press **GRAPH**, you will see the ball moving around the path where the unit circle used to be.

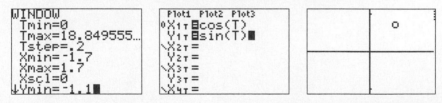

3. It might not be immediately apparent what this has to do with a ball bouncing on a spring. Change Xmin to -100 and Xmax to 100 and press **GRAPH**. The ball will follow the *same circle*, but the horizontal interval will be so large that there will be no noticeable horizontal movement. What does the vertical movement resemble?

4. Explain why the ball moves faster as it passes the origin and more slowly at the top and the bottom of its path. (*Hint*: Remember that it is really following a circular path.)

5. Would the speed of a ball on a spring vary the same way as the speed of the ball in Exercise 4?

Algebra 2 Activity 37   **77**

The Way the Ball Bounces (continued)

Exercises

1. Keep the calculator settings the same as in Exercise 3 in the Investigation, but change Tstep to .4. Explain what happens to the graph.

2. How could you change the window settings so that the ball bounces up and down six times? Test your conjecture.

3. The same bouncing motion can be used to generate a wave. Keep all the same WINDOW settings the same as in step 1 of the investigation, except change Tmax to 6π, Xmin to 0, and Xmax to 20. Then, in the Y= screen, let X1T = T and Y1T = sin(T). Change the graph style to '\'. Press GRAPH . What kind of curve do you get?

4. Now change Xmin to −5000 and Xmax to 5000. Press GRAPH . What do you see? Explain what happened to the wave.

5. In the Y= menu, change the style back to the moving ball and press GRAPH . What do you see? Explain what happened to the wave.

6. Explain in your own words the connection between the wave, the bouncing ball, and the unit circle. Now you understand harmonic motion!

Graphing Ellipses and Hyperbolas   Activity 38

The activity *The Way the Ball Bounces* illustrates how the unit circle can be graphed in parametric mode by letting X1T = cos(T) and Y1T = sin(T). In this activity you will learn how to extend this technique to graph ellipses and, with a little help from an identity, to graph hyperbolas.

Investigate

1. Make sure your calculator is in parametric ('Par') and Radian mode. In the $\boxed{Y=}$ screen, set X1T = cos(T) and Y1T = sin(T). In the $\boxed{WINDOW}$ screen, set Tmin = 0, Tmax = 2π, and Tstep = .1. Then choose $\boxed{ZOOM}$ **4 : ZDecimal** to produce the graph of the unit circle in the ZDecimal window.

2. The ellipse shown at right is just the unit circle stretched by a factor of 3 horizontally and by a factor of 2 vertically. Make simple changes to X1T and Y1T in the $\boxed{Y=}$ screen so that your calculator produces this graph.

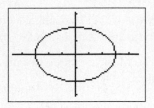

3. Let x = X1T and y = Y1T be the functions you used in step 2 to produce the graph of the ellipse. Use substitution and a well-known trig identity to show algebraically that $\dfrac{x^2}{9} + \dfrac{y^2}{4} = 1$. What horizontal and vertical stretch factors will produce the

   graph of $\dfrac{x^2}{a^2} + \dfrac{y^2}{b^2} = 1$?

4. Let $x = \dfrac{1}{\cos(T)}$ and $y = \dfrac{\sin(T)}{\cos(T)}$. Show algebraically that $x^2 - y^2 = 1$. What kind of graph does this relation produce?

5. In the $\boxed{Y=}$ screen, let X1T = $\dfrac{1}{\cos(T)}$ and Y1T = $\dfrac{\sin(T)}{\cos(T)}$. Press $\boxed{GRAPH}$. You will get a graph of the *unit hyperbola*, including its asymptotes.

Exercises

1. The function in Y1T in Exercise 5 of the investigation can be replaced by a simpler function. Name this function.

2. The graph at right shows the unit hyperbola stretched by one factor horizontally and another factor vertically, much like the ellipse was obtained from the unit circle. Use the *x*-intercepts to determine the horizontal stretch factor; then use the slopes of the asymptotes to find the vertical stretch factor.

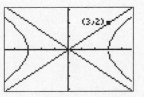

3. Make slight changes to X1T and Y1T from Exercise 5 of the investigation to produce the graph in Exercise 2.

Vertical Angles

Construct

Construct lines $\overleftrightarrow{AB}$ and $\overleftrightarrow{AC}$. Construct point D on $\overleftrightarrow{AB}$ so that A is

between D and B. Construct point E
on $\overleftrightarrow{AC}$ so that A is between C and E.

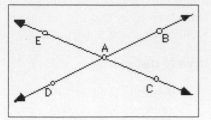

Investigate

Measure all four angles. Drag points B and C and observe the effect on the angle measures. Angles $\angle BAC$ and $\angle EAD$ are called vertical angles.

1. Make a conjecture about vertical angles.

2. Use 'Calculate' to determine the sum of ∡ EAD and EAB. Justify this result.

3. Use 'Calculate' to determine the sum of ∡ EAD and BAC. Justify this result.

4. Based on your answers to Exercises 2 and 3, what is the value of the expression $(\angle EAD + \angle EAB) - (\angle EAB + \angle BAC)$?

5. How does your result in Exercise 4 justify the conjecture made in Exercise 1?

Extend

6. Draw two pairs of vertical angles. Construct the angle bisectors of all four angles formed.

7. Make a conjecture about the angle bisectors of the two pairs of vertical angles formed by the intersection of two lines. Use 'Measure', 'Angle' and 'Calculate' to verify this conjecture.

8. **Challenge** Justify the result found in Exercise 6.

Exterior Angles of Triangles

Activity 40

Construct

Construct △*ABC* with exterior angle ∠*BCD*. ∠*A* and ∠*B* are called remote interior angles for ∠*BCD*.

Measure each angle of the triangle. Measure ∠*BCD*. Calculate the sum of ∠*A* and ∠*B*.

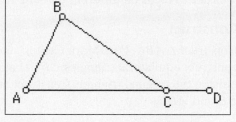

Investigate

1. Manipulate the triangle by dragging vertices to see how the relationships of the angle measures are affected. Write a conjecture about the relationship between an exterior angle and the sum of its remote interior angles.

2. What is the relationship between ∠*BCD* and ∠*BCA*? How does this relationship help justify the conclusion drawn in Exercise 1?

Extend

Construct right triangle △*ABC* with right angle ∠*B* and exterior angles ∠*CAD* and ∠*ACE*. Find the measures of ∠*BAC*, ∠*BCA* and their sum. Find the measures of ∠*CAD* and ∠*ACE* and their sum. Manipulate the triangle and observe the effect on these measures.

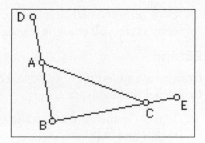

3. Make a conjecture about the sum of ∠*BAC* and ∠*BCA*. Justify your conclusion.

4. Make a conjecture about the sum of ∠*CAD* and ∠*ACE*. Use your conjecture from the first part of this activity to justify this conclusion.

Investigate Further

Construct general convex quadrilateral *ABCD* with exterior angle ∠*ADE*. Measure ∠*ADE* and calculate the sum of ∠*A*, ∠*B*, and ∠*C*.

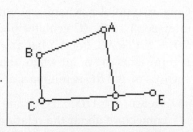

5. Use 'Calculate' to find ∠*ADE* − (∠*A* + ∠*B* + ∠*C*). Then make a conjecture about the relationship between the sum of ∠*A*, ∠*B*, and ∠*C* and exterior angle ∠*ADE*. Justify your conclusion.

6. Repeat Exercise 5 for a convex pentagon.

7. **Challenge** Complete the table below and use this information to write a rule that relates an exterior angle to the sum of the remote interior angles for any convex polygon with *n* sides.

No. of Sides	Ext. ∠	Sum of Remote Int. ∠s	Ext. ∠ − Sum of Remote Int. ∠s
3			
4			
5			
6			

Relationships in Triangles

Activity 41

Throughout this activity, it may be helpful to use color shading and thick lines to make it easier to focus on different parts of a sketch.

Construct

Construct $\triangle ABC$. Use 'Mark Center' and 'Rotate' to construct equilateral triangles $\triangle BCD$ and $\triangle CAE$ outside the original triangle. Construct and measure $\overline{BE}$ and $\overline{AD}$.

Investigate

Drag the vertices around and observe the effect on the measures of $\overline{BE}$ and $\overline{AD}$.

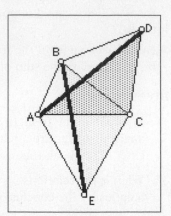

1. Make a conjecture about the relationship between $\overline{BE}$ and $\overline{AD}$.

2. Explain why $\triangle ADC \cong \triangle EBC$.

3. How does the fact that $\triangle ADC \cong \triangle EBC$ prove the conjecture you made in Exercise 1?

Extend

Construct equilateral triangle $\triangle ABF$ outside of $\triangle ABC$. Construct and measure $\overline{CF}$.

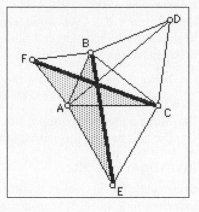

4. Make a conjecture about the relationship of $\overline{CF}$ to $\overline{BE}$ and $\overline{AD}$.

5. Using congruent triangles (shaded in diagram), explain the relationship between $\overline{CF}$ and $\overline{BE}$.

Investigate Further

Construct point S, where segments $\overline{CF}$, $\overline{BE}$, and $\overline{AD}$ intersect. Use the 'Calculator' feature to find the sum $SB + SA + SC$. Point S has an interesting property. It represents the point where the distance from S to the vertices of $\triangle ABC$ is minimized.

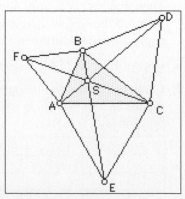

6. Measure $\angle ABS$, $\angle BSC$, and $\angle ASC$. Make a conjecture about the relationship between the measures of these three angles. Drag the vertices of $\triangle ABC$ to see if this conjecture holds.

7. Drag vertex C until point S just coincides with point B. Measure $\angle ABC$. Make a conjecture about what must be true for point S to remain within $\triangle ABC$.

8. Repeat Exercise. This time drag point S to vertices A and C. Does your conjecture still hold?

9. **Challenge** Drag point S so that it is located outside $\triangle ABC$. How is the minimum distance connecting the vertices of $\triangle ABC$ found when this happens? (*Hint:* Construct a point K not on $\triangle ABC$ and measure $KA + KB + KC$. Drag point K until this sum is minimized.)

Isosceles Triangles

Activity 42

Construct

Construct isosceles triangle $\triangle ABC$ with base $\overline{BC}$. Construct angle bisectors for $\angle ABC$ and $\angle ACB$ intersecting at D.

Investigate

1. Measure the sides and angles of $\triangle ABC$ and classify the triangle as specifically as possible.

2. Drag the vertices of $\triangle ABC$ to observe the effect on the measures. Explain why this classification holds.

3. Construct line $\overleftrightarrow{AD}$. What conclusions can be drawn about the relationship between $\overleftrightarrow{AD}$ and $\overline{BC}$?

Extend

Construct isosceles triangle $\triangle ABC$ with base $\overline{BC}$. Construct the midpoint D of $\overline{AB}$ and midpoint E of $\overline{AC}$. Construct point F on $\overline{BC}$. Construct $\overline{DF}$ and $\overline{EF}$.

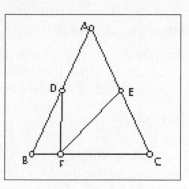

Investigate

Measure the areas of $\triangle ABC$ and quadrilateral $ADFE$. Drag the vertices of the original triangle and observe the effect on those measures.

4. Determine the relationship between the measures of the areas of $\triangle ABC$ and quadrilateral $ADFE$.

5. Consider dividing quadrilateral $ADFE$ into $\triangle ADE$ and $\triangle FDE$. How does the height of these two triangles compare with the height of $\triangle ABC$?

6. Consider $\overline{DE}$ as the base of $\triangle ADE$ and $\triangle FDE$. How does $\overline{DE}$ compare with $\overline{BC}$?

7. Use your observations in Exercises 5 and 6 to justify your conjecture in question 4.

8. Drag F so that it is the midpoint of $\overline{BC}$ and construct $\overline{DE}$. Measure the areas of the four small triangles formed. Make a conjecture about the relationships between the areas of the triangles.

9. Measure the sides of $\triangle DEF$ and $\triangle ABC$. Compare the slopes and lengths of $\overline{DE}$ with $\overline{BC}$, $\overline{DF}$ with $\overline{AC}$ and $\overline{EF}$ with $\overline{AB}$. What theorem is being demonstrated here?

10. Repeat Exercises 4 through 9 for scalene $\triangle ABC$. Do your conjectures still hold?

Orthocenters   Activity 43

Construct

Construct △ABC. Construct its three
altitudes and their point of intersection D.
This point is called the orthocenter.

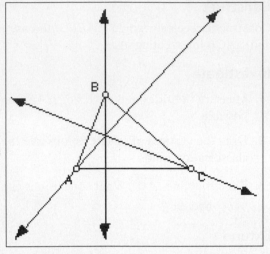

Investigate

1. Drag the vertices of △ABC. Make a
   conjecture about the types of triangles
   in which the orthocenter lies inside the
   triangle, on the triangle, or outside of
   the triangle.

Construct segments $\overline{AD}$, $\overline{BD}$, and $\overline{CD}$ and
hide lines $\overleftrightarrow{AD}$, $\overleftrightarrow{BD}$, and $\overleftrightarrow{CD}$. Find the
orthocenter of △ABD.

2. Drag △ABC and observe the effect on the orthocenter of △ABD. Make a
   conjecture about the orthocenters of △ABC, △BCD, and △ACD. Test your
   conjecture by finding the orthocenters of △BCD and △ACD.

Extend

Step 1
Use 'Point at Midpoint' and 'Perpendicular
Line' to construct the three perpendicular
bisectors of △ABC. Construct point H, the
point of intersection of these lines.

Step 2
Hide the perpendicular bisectors and
midpoints, then use 'Circle by Center +
Point' to create a circle that
circumscribes △ABC.

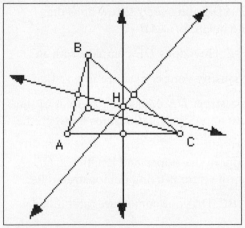

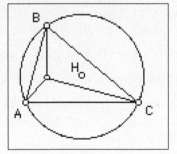

Repeat this process to construct the three circles that circumscribe the smaller triangles.

Investigate

Measure the circumference and the area of each of the four circumscribed circles. Drag
△ABC and observe the effect on the circles and on the circumferences and areas.

3. Make a conjecture about the relationships between the circle circumscribed about
   △ABC and those circumscribed about the triangles created by two of its vertices
   together with its orthocenter.

Quadrilaterals

Activity 44

Construct

Construct quadrilateral *ABCD* that is not a parallelogram, trapezoid, or kite.

Construct the midpoints of $\overline{AB}, \overline{BC}, \overline{CD},$ and $\overline{DA}$ and name them *E, F, G,* and *H*, respectively. Construct quadrilateral *EFGH*.

Measure the sides and angles of *EFGH*.

Investigate

1. Classify *EFGH* as specifically as possible. Manipulate the figure and verify that this classification holds.

2. Construct $\overline{BD}$ and determine its measure. Measure the two sides of *EFGH* that do not intersect $\overline{BD}$. How are they related? How to they relate to $\overline{BD}$?

3. Use your answers from Exercise 2 to justify the conclusion made in Exercise 1.

4. Repeat Exercises 1 through 3 with *IJKL*, a quadrilateral formed by joining the midpoints of *EFGH*. Classify *IJKL* as specifically as possible. Manipulate the figure and verify that this classification holds.

5. Construct rhombus *ABCD* and its midpoints *E, F, G,* and *H*. Construct and classify *EFGH* as specifically as possible. Manipulate the figure and verify that this classification holds.

6. Explain how the slopes of diagonals $\overline{BD}$ and $\overline{AC}$ can be used to verify the conclusion drawn in Exercise 5.

7. Construct rectangle *ABCD* and its midpoints *E, F, G,* and *H*. Construct and classify *EFGH* as specifically as possible. Manipulate the figure and verify that this classification holds.

8. Repeat Exercise 7 for square *ABCD*.

9. Repeat Exercise 7 for isosceles trapezoid *ABCD*.

10. Repeat Exercise 7 for kite *ABCD*.

11. Make a conjecture about the properties a quadrilateral must have so that the figure formed by joining consecutive midpoints is a rhombus.

12. Make a conjecture about the properties a quadrilateral must have so that the figure formed by joining consecutive midpoints is a rectangle.

13. Explain why the midpoints of a quadrilateral will never form a kite or an isosceles trapezoid.

Using Different Menus to Construct Special Quadrilaterals

Activity 45

Construct

Here is one way to construct a kite.

Draw segment $\overline{AB}$ with point C on $\overline{AB}$. Construct a line through C perpendicular to $\overline{AB}$. Place point E on this line and construct a circle with radius $\overline{CE}$. Construct point F, the intersection of $\overleftrightarrow{CE}$ and $\odot C$.

Measure the sides of $AEBF$ and verify that the quadrilateral is a kite.

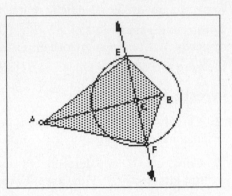

Investigate

Here are two more ways to construct a kite.

1. Construct acute $\triangle ABC$. Use 'Mark Mirror' and 'Reflect' to reflect $\triangle ABC$ about one of its sides. Hide the segment that was marked to create a quadrilateral. Drag the vertices and verify the quadrilateral is a kite. Identify the property of a kite makes this construction work. Explain.

2. Construct $\odot A$ and $\odot C$, intersecting at points B and D. Construct radii $\overline{AB}, \overline{AD}, \overline{BC},$ and $\overline{CD}$. Hide the circles. Identify the property of a kite that makes this construction work. Explain.

Investigate Further

Complete each construction. Name the resulting quadrilateral as specifically as possible. Identify the properties of quadrilaterals that make each construction work. Explain.

3. Draw $\odot F$. Construct diameters $\overline{AC}$ and $\overline{BD}$. Construct segments $\overline{AB}, \overline{BC}, \overline{CD}$, and $\overline{AD}$.

4. Construct a right triangle. Use 'Mark Center' and 'Rotate' to create the same quadrilateral in Exercise 3.

5. Construct an isosceles triangle. Use 'Mark Mirror' and 'Reflect' to reflect the triangle over its base.

6. Construct a circle with two radii. Use 'Parallel line' to construct segments parallel to each radius.

Extend

Step 1 Draw segment $\overline{AB}$ with midpoint E. Separately, draw $\angle XYZ$.

Step 2 Highlight point E and select 'Mark Center'. Highlight points $X, Y,$ and Z, making sure that Y is the second point you highlight, and select 'Mark Angle'.

Step 3 Highlight $\overline{AB}$ (including the endpoints) and select 'Rotate'. Make sure that the 'By marked angle' button is selected. Name this new segment $\overline{CD}$.

Step 4 Construct segments $\overline{AD}, \overline{DB}, \overline{BC},$ and $\overline{AC}$. Manipulate $ADBC$ by dragging one of its vertices or by dragging point X or Z on $\angle XYZ$. Identify quadrilateral $ABCD$. Name the property of that quadrilateral that makes this construction work. Explain.

Parallelograms and Triangles

Activity 46

Construct

Step 1

Construct parallelogram *ABCD* and line $\overleftrightarrow{AB}$. Then construct a circle with radius $\overline{AD}$. Construct point *F* where the circle and line $\overleftrightarrow{AB}$ intersect. Choose point *F* so that *A* is between *F* and *B*. This ensures that $AF = AD$.

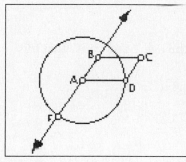

Step 2

Hide the circle with center *A*. In a similar manner, construct a circle with radius $\overline{BC}$ and point *E* on $\overleftrightarrow{AB}$ so that *B* is between *A* and *E*.

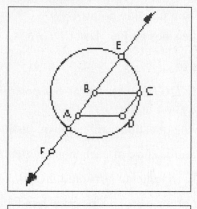

Step 3

Hide circle *B*. Then construct $\overleftrightarrow{FD}$ and $\overleftrightarrow{EC}$ intersecting at point *H*. Your diagram should look like the diagram at right.

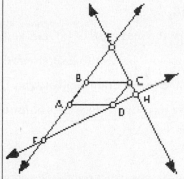

Investigate

1. Find the measures of all angles in parallelogram *ABCD* and in △*EFH*.

2. Drag the vertices of the parallelogram and observe the effect on the angle measures. Make a conjecture about the relationship between ∠*BAD* and ∠*AFD* as well as ∠*ABC* and ∠*BEC*.

3. Use properties of isosceles triangles, supplements, and the sum of the angles of a triangle to justify your conjecture in Exercise 1.

4. Find the sum of the measures of ∠*BEC* and ∠*AFD*. Based on your observations, make a conjecture about *m*∠*CHD*.

5. Measure ∠*HCD* and ∠*CDH*. Make a conjecture about how the measures of these angles compare with the measures of ∠*BEC* and ∠*AFD*.

6. What property of parallel lines justifies your conjecture in Exercise 5?

Regular Polygons

Activity 47

Construct

Construct points *A* and *B*. Using *A* as a center of rotation, rotate the image of *B* 72°. Repeat until the image point is concurrent with the original point *B*. Connect the points in the order in which they were created to form regular pentagon *BCDEF*.

Construct diagonals $\overline{DB}$ and $\overline{CF}$ and label their point of intersection *G*. Hide point *A*.

Measure the sides and angles of *DGFE*.

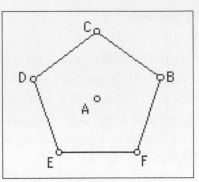

Investigate

1. Classify *DGFE* as specifically as possible. Manipulate the figure and verify that this classification holds.

The following questions will help you justify the result found in Exercise 1.

2. Find the measure of each angle of pentagon *BCDEF*.

3. Classify triangles △*DBC* and △*CFB*.

4. Use your answers to Exercises 2 and 3 to determine the measures of ∡*CDB* and *CFB*.

5. What are the measures of ∡*GDE* and *GFE*? angle *E*?

6. Based on your answer to Exercise 5, find the measure of ∠*DGF*?

7. Determine the relationship between $\overline{DE}$ and $\overline{EF}$.

8. Use your answers to Exercises 5 through 7 to justify the conclusion found in Exercise 1.

Extend

Use rotations to construct regular hexagon *ABCDEF* with diagonals $\overline{AD}$ and $\overline{BE}$ intersecting at *G*.

9. Classify *AGEF* as specifically as possible. Manipulate the figure and verify that this classification holds.

10. Construct a regular heptagon. Draw two diagonals that produce the same quadrilateral.

11. Repeat Exercise 10 for a regular octagon.

12. Make a conjecture as to how to draw diagonals of regular polygons in order to produce the type of quadrilateral formed in this activity.

Area

Activity 48

Construct

Step 1 Construct segment $\overline{AD}$. Use 'Mark Center "A"' to rotate $\overline{AD}$ 90°. Label the new point B. Use a similar procedure to complete the construction of square $ABCD$.

Step 2 Draw two segments from vertex A to point E on side $\overline{BC}$ and to point F on side $\overline{CD}$.

Investigate

Measure the areas of $\triangle ABE$, $AECF$, and $\triangle AFD$. Drag E and F until the three regions formed have equal area; that is, the area of the square has been trisected.

1. Calculate the ratios $\dfrac{BE}{EC}$ and $\dfrac{DF}{FC}$. Drag the vertices of the square and make a conjecture about the areas and their relationship to the ratios.

2. Use the formula for the area of a triangle, $A = \frac{1}{2}bh$, to justify why this result works as it does. (Hint: Label side AB as $3x$, then label each of the segments along $\overline{BC}$ and $\overline{CD}$ in terms of x. Find the areas of $\triangle ABE$ and AFD in terms of x as well as the area of $ABCD$. This should provide enough information to show that the area of $ABCD$ has been trisected.)

Extend

3. Construct square $ABCD$ with segments $\overline{AE}$, $\overline{AF}$, and $\overline{AG}$ as shown in the diagram at right. Measure the areas of the four resulting regions. Drag E, F, and G so that the four regions have equal area.

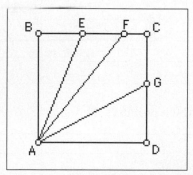

4. Measure the lengths of the segments along $\overline{BC}$ and $\overline{CD}$ and calculate their ratios with one another. Make a conjecture about the position of E, F, and G.

5. Use the formula for the area of a triangle, $A = \frac{1}{2}bh$, to justify why this result works as it does.

6. Repeat Exercises 3 through 5 by dividing square $ABCD$ into five regions with equal area.

7. Repeat Exercises 3 through 5 by dividing square $ABCD$ into six regions with equal area.

8. Make a conjecture as to how to position segments when dividing a square into an even number of regions with equal area.

9. Make a conjecture as to how to position segments when dividing a square into an odd number of regions with equal area.

Pythagorean Triples

Activity 49

The Pythagorean Theorem states that for every right triangle with legs of lengths a and b and hypotenuse of length c, the formula $a^2 + b^2 = c^2$ is always true.

If a, b, and c are integers, then the three numbers a, b, and c are called a Pythagorean triple. For example, the numbers 3, 4, and 5 are a Pythagorean triple because $3^2 + 4^2 = 9 + 16 = 25 = 5^2$. Many mathematicians were fascinated by Pythagorean triples and were interested in finding algorithms that produce Pythagorean triples.

Here are some of their formulas for generating triples:

Masere's method: $m^2 - n^2, 2mn, m^2 + n^2$, where m and n are positive integers with $m > n$;

Plato's method: $\frac{n^2}{4} - 1, n, \frac{n^2}{4} + 1$, where n is an even integer greater than 2;

Pythagoras: $\frac{(n^2 - 1)}{2}, n, \frac{(n^2 + 1)}{2}$, where n is an odd integer greater than 1;

Unattributed: $2n + 1, 2n^2 + 2n, 2n^2 + 2n + 1$, where n is an integer greater than 0.

Investigate

A spreadsheet can be used to generate a list of Pythagorean triples using the formulas given above. Masere's method is shown here with the first four sets of Pythagorean triples.

Masere's method uses the formulas

m	n	$m^2 - n^2$	$2mn$	$m^2 + n^2$
2	1	= A2*A2 − B2*B2	= 2*A2*B2	= A2*A2 + B2*B2
= A2 + 1	= B2 + 1	= A3*A3 − B3*B3	= 2*A3*B3	= A3*A3 + B3*B3
= A3 + 1	= B3 + 1	= A4*A4 − B4*B4	= 2*A4*B4	= A4*A4 + B4*B4
= A4 + 1	= B4 + 1	= A5*A5 − B5*B5	= 2*A5*B5	= A5*A5 + B5*B5

which produces the following triples.

m	n	$m^2 - n^2$	$2mn$	$m^2 + n^2$
2	1	3	4	5
3	2	5	12	13
4	3	7	24	25
5	4	9	40	41

1. Use a spreadsheet to generate a list of Pythagorean triples by Plato's method.

2. Use a spreadsheet to generate a list of Pythagorean triples by Pythagoras' method.

3. Use a spreadsheet to generate a list of Pythagorean triples using the formulas $2n + 1, 2n^2 + 2n, 2n^2 + 2n + 1$.

4. **Writing** Discuss similarities or differences between these methods.

Similarity

Construct

Construct parallelogram *ABCD* whose diagonals intersect at *E*. Measure its sides and angles. Construct the midpoints of $\overline{AE}$, $\overline{BE}$, $\overline{CE}$, and $\overline{DE}$ called *P, Q, R,* and *S*, respectively.

Construct quadrilateral *PQRS* and measure its sides and angles.

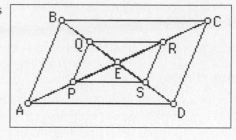

Investigate

1. Drag the vertices of *ABCD* and observe the effect on *PQRS*. Classify *PQRS* as specifically as possible.

2. Explain why this classification holds.

3. Comparing corresponding angles and sides, verify that *ABCD* and *PQRS* are similar.

4. Find the similarity ratio. Without measuring, make a conjecture about the ratio of the areas of the two figures. Test your conjecture by measuring.

5. Do you think the results in Exercises 1 through 4 are true for quadrilaterals that are not parallelograms? Test your answer by constructing and measuring.

Extend

Step 1

Construct quadrilateral *ABCD* with point *V* not on *ABCD*. Construct line segments from each vertex of *ABCD* to *V*. Construct the midpoints of $\overline{AV}$, $\overline{BV}$, $\overline{CV}$, and $\overline{DV}$, called *M, N, O,* and *P*, respectively. Point *V* is called the vanishing point.

Step 2

Draw segments connecting the corresponding vertices of *ABCD* to *MNOP*. Then hide the segments joining the vertices of *ABCD* to *V*. The three dimensional object that results is an example of a drawing in one point perspective.

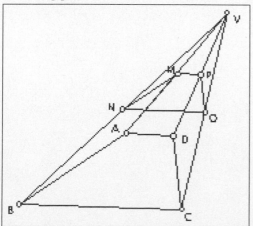

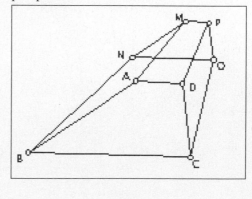

6. Measure the sides and angles of *ABCD* and *MNOP* and verify that the quadrilaterals are similar.

Similarity (continued)

7. Use your results from the investigation to determine how the area of *ABCD* compares with the area of *MNOP*. Test your conjecture by measuring the areas of both polygons.

8. Create an original sketch in one-point perspective.

Investigate Further

Two perspective drawing gives objects an even more realistic look. Construct $\overline{AB}$ and $\overline{IJ}$. Then, complete the two point perspective drawing as shown in Figure 1. Use the segment tool and the 'Hide' feature to remove lines as shown in Figure 2.

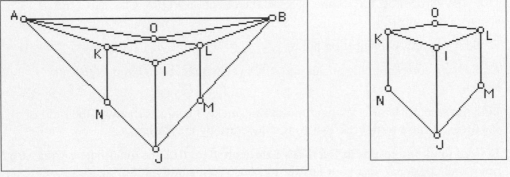

Figure 1   Figure 2

9. Identify two pairs of similar figures located in the two point perspective drawing shown in Figure 2. (Hint: Draw $\overline{AM}$ and $\overline{BN}$ intersecting at *P*. Then construct $\overline{OP}$.)

10. How do you determine the scale factor for each pair of similar figures?

11. Create an original sketch in two point perspective.

Volume

Activity 51

A shipping company requires that the maximum size of a package, defined by the distance around the girth plus the height, to be 12 ft. Suppose you are sending a box which is a square prism. Which dimensions maximize the volume of the package? What is the maximum volume?

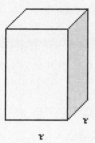

Investigate

1. Let x represent the length and width of the base. Determine the height of the prism in terms of x.

2. Write an equation, $V(x)$, for the volume of the prism.

Enter your equation for the volume of the prism as Y1 in the graphing calculator. Set the table so that TblStart = .25 (0.25 ft or 3 in.) and $\triangle$Tbl = .25.

3. Scroll down the table and identify the value of x that maximizes the volume.

4. Use the **TRACE** or [CALC] **4 : maximum** feature to confirm the result found in question 3. What is the maximum volume?

Sometimes it is important to consider the surface area of a package as well as its volume.

5. Write an equation, $S(x)$, that represents the surface area for the prism defined in question 1.

6. Graph $S(x)$ as Y2 and determine the dimensions of the prism that maximize the surface area.

7. Are the dimensions that maximize the surface area the same dimensions that maximize the volume?

8. Consider a situation where the surface area cannot exceed 30 square feet. Graph the horizontal line Y3 = 30 along with Y1 and Y2. Use the [CALC] **5 : intersect** feature to determine the points of intersection of Y2 and Y3. Which point yields the largest volume? Determine the volume at this point.

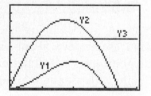

Extend

Suppose you are shipping a cylindrical container whose volume is given by $V = \pi r^2 h$ where r is the radius and h is the height. Again, consider that the distance around the girth plus the height must be 12 ft.

9. Write an equation $V(x)$, where x represents the radius, that describes the volume of this container.

10. Graph the equation found in Exercise 1 as Y1. Which dimensions maximize the volume of this package? What is the maximum volume?

11. Write an equation, $S(x)$, that represents the surface area for the cylinder.

12. Graph $S(x)$ as Y2 and determine the dimensions of the cylinder that maximize the surface area.

13. **Writing** Explain why a shipping company must consider several variables, such as volume, surface area, and maximum size when establishing delivery prices.

Rotations

Activity 52

Construct

Construct points *A* and *B*. Using *A* as a center of rotation, rotate *B* 60°. Rotate the image of *B* 60°. Repeat until the image point is concurrent with the original point *B*. Connect the points in the order in which they were created.

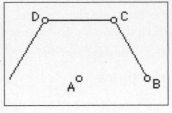

Investigate

1. Measure sides and angles, then classify the polygon.

Repeat the activity above, this time rotating by 90°. Connect the points in the order in which they were created.

2. Measure sides and angles, then classify the polygon.

Repeat the activity above, this time rotating by 100° four times.

3. Make a conjecture about why the last point does not coincide with the first point.

4. Make a conjecture about the whole number rotations that will produce regular polygons. Give three examples and construct those polygons.

Extend

5. Measure ∠*BCD* of the original polygon. Make a conjecture as to how this angle relates to the angle of rotation used to construct the polygon.

6. Does your conjecture from Exercise 1 hold true for the other polygons you were able to construct?

7. Draw a line segment from point A to each of the vertices of the original construction. How does this help you prove your conjecture from Exercise 1?

By using 'Mark Mirror' and 'Reflect' from the 'Transform' menu, create several copies of the original polygon. This polygon forms a tessellation, a pattern of shapes that fill a plane without any overlap or gaps.

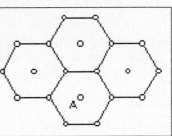

8. Name another polygon from the investigation that you think will form a tessellation.

9. Make a conjecture as to why certain polygons tessellate and others do not.

As can be seen from the diagram at right, a regular octagon cannot be used to form a tessellation. However, a combination of squares and regular octagons will form what is called a *semi-pure tessellation*.

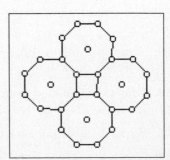

10. Explain why the square and regular octagon can be combined to form a semi-pure tessellation.

11. Find and construct one other pair of polygons that form a semi-pure tessellation.

Using the Web to Study Mathematics

The world wide web contains a vast array of information, some of which is useful and some that is not. *Search engines* are used to help you find information on the web, but it is up to you to decide if the sites your search produces are meaningful and valid. A good search can help you locate a store, find the meaning of a word or phrase, answer a question about mathematics, and even purchase a car.

In this activity, you will explore a chapter of your textbook, search the web for math help sites, and generate a help sheet for your classmates.

Activity Directions

Step 1 Divide into pairs. Using your textbook, explore a chapter you are about to begin and find five main topics in the chapter.

Step 2 Share your choices with the rest of the class and, as a group, determine the top four topics.

Step 3 Use a search engine to find two math help sites. Your browser's homepage, such as http://www.netscape.com or http://www.msn.com, has search capabilities. You can also go to a specific search engine home page, such as http://www.google.com or http://www.looksmart.com, to begin your search.

Tips about using a search engine

General, you can just enter a few descriptive words about the topic you want to search. Most search engines ignore words such as 'the', 'how', 'where', as well as single digits or letters.

You also do not need to include the word 'and' between two words. For example, 'fractions decimals' will generally produce the same results as 'fractions and decimals'. In both cases, your search will find pages that contain both of these words.

The phrase 'fractions or decimals' will find pages that contain the key words 'fractions' or 'decimals', whether they occur separately or together.

If you are looking for the exact match for a phrase, enclose your entire entry in double quotation marks. For example, "Do not be troubled by your difficulties with Mathematics, I can assure you mine are much greater." will appear together in all returned documents exactly as you have entered them.

Some search engines also allow you to use the asterisk (*) wild card character to find different branches of a word. For example, 'equa*' will help you find 'equation', 'equality', 'equilibrium', etc.

Step 4 Once you have found your two math help sites, find two questions with answers for each topic. Write down the questions and answers.

Step 5 When each group is finished, divide into four teams, one for each topic. Type up a single page that has all of the questions and answers about that topic. On a separate page, describe any similarities you may have noticed about the problems you found. Also include an explanation as to how you can avoid problems you or your classmates had with this topic.

Step 6 Share your findings with the class and submit the typewritten sheets to your teacher.

Mining Data Found on the Internet

The Internet is the source of an almost unlimited amount of data. When searching for data, it is important to look for web sites that are dependable. Web sites created by government agencies, high profile companies or organizations, and educational institutions generally contain information that is accurate, up to date, and reliable.

In this activity, you will conduct Internet searches for the purpose of finding data that relates two variables (such as average height and age). You will then *mine* the data, meaning you will look for patterns and relationships contained within the data. Finally, you will present the data in written, graphical, or algebraic form.

Activity Directions

Throughout this activity, you will be using search techniques to locate information on the Internet. Refer to the web-based activity "Using the Web to Study Mathematics" for tips on how to search the Internet effectively.

Step 1 Working individually or in small groups, search the Internet for data on the winning times for the Women's Olympic 4 × 100-meter Freestyle Relay during the summer Olympics. In table form, record the winning times for the years 1952–1992.

Step 2 Using graph paper or a spreadsheet program, create a scatter plot that plots the year versus winning times for the data you collected. Determine if there is a linear relationship between the year and winning times.

Step 3 Draw a line of best fit that models the data and determine the equation of the line. Remember that the line of best fit does not need to contain the actual data points.

Step 4 Use the equation of the line of best fit to predict the winning time for the women's 4 × 100-meter relay during the Atlanta summer Olympics in 1996. Check your Internet source to see how close the prediction was. Explain any differences between the predicted time and the actual winning time.

Exercise

Choose a topic that may interest you and search that Internet for data relating to this topic. You should look for data that relates two or more variables. For example, you may choose to explore relationships between the heights and weights of professional athletes. This information is readily available on the Internet. Other possible data types include:

• Population statistics
• Economic, business, or employment trends
• Weather data

Once you have decided on a topic, follow steps 1 through 4 of the activity directions. If the data does not show a linear relationship, look other types of relationships that might exist. Create a display and present your findings to the rest of the class.

Generating Quizzes on the Web

There are several web sites that offer on-line quizzes. One such web site, located at http://www.quia.com, allows you to create your own quizzes, activities, and games which are then posted on the web for others to use.

In this activity, you will create two quizzes, one for Algebra 1 students and another for use with your Algebra 2 class.

Activity Directions

Step 1 Divide into pairs. Write an integer quiz with at least 10 questions that includes addition, subtraction, multiplication, and division using only integers from −20 to 20. Construct the quiz so that the answers are also integers from −20 to 20.

Step 2 Go to http://www.quia.com and click on the 'First Time User' button. You will be prompted to enter your username, password, name, and email address. Your teacher can provide you with an email address and username if you do not have one. Make sure that you write down your username and password; you will be required to enter this information next time you log on. Click the 'Create my account' button.

Step 3 Select 'matching, flashcard, concentration, word search' from the pull down menu and click 'GO'. On the next screen, you are prompted to fill out 7 sections to create your activity. Section 2 contains the questions—the first column should contain the problem and the second column contains the answer. Set up the activity for flashcards and matching.

Step 4 When you are finished creating the activity, click the 'submit' button. On the next screen you will be given the URL address for your activity. Make sure that you record this address and give it to your teacher. Your activities are also listed in your account each time you log in.

Step 5 Test the activity you have just created and verify that it works correctly.

Step 6 Create a new game using information from your Algebra 2 textbook. Here's a brief description of the activities from which to choose:

- Matching, Flashcard, Concentration, Word Search: Can be used for most short answer questions or vocabulary. Word search should only be used for vocabulary.

- Challenge Board: Organizes questions by category and point value, much like a popular game show on TV!

- Hangman: Used for vocabulary words only

- Jumbled Words: Used for vocabulary words/definitions only

- Ordered Lists: Answers must be entered from least to greatest or greatest to least.

- Picture Perfect: Answers must be entered from least to greatest or greatest to least. A picture is revealed if the order is correct.

- Pop Ups: Sentences (English or mathematical) are completed by selecting the correct choice from a pull down menu.

- Rags to Riches: Multiple choice

- Scavenger Hunt: Internet links are given that provide answers to each question. Well suited for terms and definitions.

Graphing the Solar System

In the early 1600s, Johannes Kepler discovered that the orbit of Mars was an ellipse with one focus centered at the sun. This observation was eventually extended to all the planets and given the name "Kepler's First Law".

As you are aware, an ellipse is a set of points in a plane such that the sum of the distances from any point to two fixed points (called foci) is constant. Three of the main components of an ellipse are its major axis, minor axis, and foci. Another characteristic of an ellipse is its eccentricity, e, which can be calculated by the formula $e = \frac{c}{a}$. The eccentricity of an ellipse, which is a number that lies between 0 and 1, is used to describe how nearly circular the ellipse is.

In this activity, you will research information about the planets and use what you know about ellipses to create a scale model of the orbits of the planets in our solar system. You will also create a second poster, showing a scale drawing representing the sizes of the planets.

Investigation

You will start by determining the equation and graph of Saturn's orbit. All units will be written in astronomical units (AU). One AU is equal to the average distance from the Sun to Earth, which is about 93,000,000 miles.

1. The average distance from Saturn to the Sun is 887 million miles. This number represents the value of a for a horizontal ellipse whose equation is represented by $\frac{x^2}{a^2} + \frac{y^2}{b^2} = 1$. Convert a to astronomical units.

2. Saturn's eccentricity, e, is 0.056. Find c.

3. Find b and the equation of the ellipse that describes Saturn's orbit.

4. Rewrite the equation in the form $\frac{(x + c)^2}{a^2} + \frac{y^2}{b^2} = 1$. The equation of the ellipse in this form will position the Sun at the origin.

5. To graph the ellipse found in step 4, solve the equation for y and enter it into your graphing calculator (you will need to graph the ellipse as two pieces since it doesn't represent a function). Use the square window shown at right. You will notice that there are breaks in the ellipse near the x-axis.

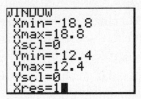

```
WINDOW
Xmin=-18.8
Xmax=18.8
Xscl=0
Ymin=-12.4
Ymax=12.4
Yscl=0
Xres=1█
```

6. Based on the graph, you may think that the orbit of the planet Saturn is a circle, but it is not. Explain. Relate your answer to the eccentricity of the ellipse and the location of the foci.

Activity

Step 1 With a partner, search the web for planetary data on Mercury, Venus, Earth and Mars. These planets are called the *terrestrial* or *rocky* planets.

Step 2 Follow steps 1 through 4 in the investigation above to find the equation of the ellipse that describes each of these planets.

Step 3 Graph each orbit in the same viewing window. Make sure that you choose a square window that allows the largest orbit to fill the viewing window.

Graphing the Solar System (continued)

Step 4 On a poster board with graph paper, sketch a graph of the orbits of the four terrestrial planets. Use `TRACE` or `2nd` [TABLE] to find specific points on each graph. Include a title, labels, and equations on the poster. This will give an approximate model as to how the planetary orbits relate to one another.

Step 5 The orbits of Jupiter, Saturn, Uranus, and Neptune (called the jovian or gas planets) are much larger than the terrestrial planets. Repeat steps 1–4 for the Jovian Planets. Sketch the graph of the orbits of the jovian planets on the reverse side of your poster board.

Step 6 Search the web for information on each of the nine planets (including Pluto). On a separate poster board, create a scale drawing of the planets. Include data for each planet such as mass, diameter, length of day, moons, etc.

Exercises

1. Explain why it is difficult to show a scale drawing of all nine planets on the same graph.

2. How large do you think your sketch would need to be in order to reasonably see the orbits of all nine planets?

3. Determine the equation that models the orbit of Pluto.

4. The average distance from Pluto to the Sun is 3.7 billion miles, compared with the next farthest planet, Neptune, with an average distance of about 3 billion miles. Despite this difference in average distance, Pluto is sometimes closer to the sun than Neptune. Search the web for more information about the orbits of Pluto and Neptune and explain why this happens.

5. On July 4, 2001, Earth reached the aphelion, its farthest distance from Earth to the Sun. In the Northern Hemisphere, however, the climate on this date was much warmer than the climate on January 4, 2001 when Earth reached the perihelion, its closest distance to the Sun. Search the web for information related to this idea and explain why this phenomenon happens.

6. Explain why it is important for Earth's orbit to be nearly circular.

Building a Web Page About Buildings

In this activity, you will create a web page that includes images of buildings containing a variety of geometric shapes. This activity can be completed individually but is best suited for small groups. You will need a computer (Macintosh or PC) and a connection to the Internet.

Activity Directions

Step 1 Open a text editor program on your computer. If you are using a Macintosh computer, the application *SimpleText,* which comes free with the system, will work fine. On a PC, you can use the application *Notepad.*

Step 2 Type the following code, exactly as it appears below, in your text editor document. Do not type the information contained within curly braces ({ }) – these contain comments that describe what each line means.

```
<html>                                {indicates that this file is written in HTML language}
<head>                {the prelude of the document is contained between the <head> tags}
<title> Team Geometry Web Page </title>                            {the document title}
</head>                                                    {end of document prelude}
<body bgcolor="black" text="yellow">                           {start of body of page, sets
                                                     background color and text color}
<img src="image1">                         {places image called "image1" on page}
<p>                                                       {starts a new paragraph}
Text about picture 1.                             {words to describe "image1"}
</p>                                                          {end of paragraph}
<img src="image2">                         {places image called "image2" on page}
<p>                                                       {starts a new paragraph}
Text about picture 2.                             {words to describe "image2"}
</p>                                                          {end of paragraph}
<img src="image3">                         {places image called "image3" on page}
<p>                                                       {starts a new paragraph}
Text about picture 3.                             {words to describe "image3"}
</p>                                                          {end of paragraph}
<img src="image4">                         {places image called "image4" on page}
<p>                                                       {starts a new paragraph}
Text about picture 4.                             {words to describe "image4"}
</p>                                                          {end of paragraph}
</body>                                                {end of body of document}
</html>                                                 {end of HTML document}
```

Step 3 Now that you have finished typing the html code for your web page, save the file by clicking on 'File' and 'Save As'. Create a new folder called *World Geometry* and save the file as *index.html*. The suffix 'html' must be included because is tells your web browser that this is a web page.

Building a Web Page About Buildings (continued)

Step 4 Open *Netscape* or *Internet Explorer* and click on 'File' and 'Open'. Open the World Geometry folder and select the file index.html. Your web page should appear in your browser window (if not, doublecheck each line of the program).

****Step 5** It should be no surprise that pictures are missing. Your next responsibility is to search the web for pictures of interesting buildings in four cities from around the world. When you find a picture of an interesting building, study it. Find the number of geometric figures that are contained in it.

Step 6 You will also need to save your four pictures to the World Geometry folder. On a Macintosh, click and hold your mouse on the picture you wish to save and select 'download image to disk'. Make sure that you change the names of each picture to *image1, image2, ..., image4*. Write down the web site where you found each picture and the cities in which they are located.

Step 7 When you have saved all four pictures go back to your *Notepad* or *SimpleText* document and delete the lines that say "Text for image…". Replace each of these lines with a detailed description of the geometric figures you found in each picture. You must also give credit to the web site where you found each picture, and remember to list the city where each building is located.

Step 8 If you saved the pictures in the same folder location as index.html you can now use *Netscape* or *Internet Explorer* to open the page and view your group's completed web page. Once again, you will need to carefully doublecheck each line of code if the web page does not look right.

Congratulations! You may now present your findings to the rest of the class.

Keep in mind that you may not post your site on the Internet until you have written permission from the source sites indicating that you can use their images on your own site.

Extend

Research the Internet or check your local library to learn more about html programming. Try to add additional features to your web page such as lists, links to related sites, different types of fonts or characters, and a new page layout. You'll be surprised how easy it is to make enhancements to your web page!

** Check this out on a PC.

Creating Dynamic Images for the Web

If you have surfed the web in the past, you have inevitably come across an image of an object that transforms (or morphs) itself into another object. This type of animation is created by special state of the art software, capable of giving web pages a dynamic, eye-catching look without the requirement of long downloads. The word *tween* is used to describe this type of animation and a software product called *Macromedia Flash* is one program that can create such tweens.

In the activity below, you will use *Macromedia Flash* to create an animation where two parallel lines tween into two perpendicular lines.

Activity

Step 1 If your computer lab is not equipped with a copy of Macromedia Flash, go the http://www.macromedia.com/downloads/ and download a 30-day free trial version.

Make sure that you have obtained permission to download the software beforehand.

Step 2 Open Macromedia Flash. Double-click on 'Layer 1' and re-name it 'Line 1'. Go to the 'Tools' at left and click on the segment tool. Draw a segment in the worksheet.

Step 3 Click on 'Insert' and 'Layer' to create a second layer. Rename the layer 'Line 2' and draw a second line just <u>below</u> the first line while 'Line 2' is still highlighted.

Step 4 Go to 'Tools', select the 'arrow tool', and highlight line 1. Select 'Insert' , 'Convert to Symbol', and press the return key. Repeat for the second line.

Step 5 Click on frame 15 of the timeline for 'Line 1'. Select 'Insert' and 'Keyframe'. Repeat this process for 'Line 2' except locate the keyframe in frame 30 rather than 15.

Step 6 Highlight the box between frames 1 and 15 of the timeline for 'Line 1' and click on 'Insert' and 'Create Motion Tween'. Click on frame 15 and drag the first line down to the second line.

Step 7 Insert a keyframe in frame 30 of 'Line 1' and create a motion tween in the box between frames 15 and 30 of 'Line 1'. Click frame 30 of 'Line 1' and select 'Windows', 'Panel' and 'Transform' to open the transform dialog box (if the transform box is not already open). Select the 'Constrain' box and make sure the 'Rotate' button is selected. Type 90° for the angle of rotation and press return.

Step 8 View the tween by clicking on 'Control' and 'Rewind', then 'Control' and 'Play'. You should see the first line move to the second line, then rotate 90°.

Creating Dynamic Images for the Web (continued)

Exercises

1. Create a tween that transforms a circle inscribed in a square into a square inscribed in a circle. You will use two layers, one for the square and the other for the circle. It will help to open the 'transform' dialog box and click on the info tab to set the size of each object (located in 'Window', 'Panels', 'Transform'). Then, create a motion tween that increases the size of the circle by a factor of $\sqrt{2} \approx 1.414$ while leaving the square unchanged. Make sure that the circle is converted to a symbol.

2. Create a rectangle of any color whose length and width are in a ratio of 4 to 3. Create a motion tween that dilates this rectangle by a scale factor of 12.

Extend

A different type of tween, called a *shape tween,* is used to transform one type of shape into a completely different shape. Unlike the motion tween, shape tweens only work on objects that are <u>not</u> symbols. To create a shape tween, draw two objects at the beginning and end of a frame. Double-click the beginning of the frame to open a dialog box. Click on the 'frame' tab. Click on the pull down menu labeled 'tweening' and select 'shape'. Select 'Control' and 'Play' to see the first object transform into the second object.

3. Create a tween that transforms a blue circle into a green square. Use the procedure described above to tween the blue circle into a blue square. Then, create a new scene that takes the blue square and changes the color to green. This can be done by creating a motion tween and using the 'Effect' panel.

4. Create a tween that transforms an orange isosceles trapezoid into a yellow kite.

For a tutorial in how to tween objects in Flash go to http://www.flashkit.com/tutorials/Getting_Started/Shape_Tw-Douglas_-547/more3.shtml or http://animation.about.com/library/weekly/blflashtutorial2a.htm. You can also select 'Help', 'Lessons', and '08 Animation' to learn about the techniques used in this activity.

Answers

Take a Walk, Part 1   Activity 1

1. **a.** 12 ft; 2 s
   b. 8 ft; 3 s
2. Check student's work.
3. Walk at a constant speed away from the motion detector.
4. Check student's work.
5. Divide the change in distance by the change in time; ft/s
6. Check student's work.
7. The speed equals the slope of the line;
   $$\text{slope} = \frac{\text{vertical change}}{\text{horizontal change}}.$$
8. a line with a steeper slope
9. Students should sketch a line with a steeper slope
10. Students should sketch a line with a less steep slope.
11–12. Check student's work.
13. Walk toward the motion detector.
14. Stand still; impossible, because the person would have to be in two places at the same time.
15. the initial distance from the motion detector
16a. stood still, then walked at a constant speed away from the detector, then stood still again
16b. walked away from the detector at a constant speed, stood still, walked toward the detector at a faster, constant speed
16c. walked away from the detector at a constant speed, stood still, walked away from the detector at a much faster, constant speed
17. Yes; the distance at the beginning and end of the graph is the same.
18. Toward the detector; the steepness is greater so the speed is greater.

Take a Walk, Part 2   Activity 2

1. negative; positive
2. the line through A; 6
3. yes; $y = 6x$
4. Check students' work.
5. Check students' work; initial distance from the motion detector
6–8. Check students' work.
9–10. Check students' work. If an equation models the data well, the line should overlap the plot. If an equation does not model the data well, the line may either have a different slope or an incorrect y–intercept.
11. The model will predict reasonable values for $x > 0$ and $x <$ the final time measured by the CBL 2 unit. Other values of x predict values before or after the student was walking.
12–14. Check students' work.
15. No; the y–intercept will be negative and does not represent the initial distance from the motion detector to the student, because the student stood still for 2 s.
16. Yes; the slope is the speed of the student after he or she began walking.

Synchronized Strut   Activity 3

1. Lines have different positive slopes and have the same y–intercept.
2. parallel with different y-intercepts
3. Same line
4–5. Check students' work.
6. y–intercept; represents initial distance from the motion detector
7–9. Check students' work.
10. Speed each student walks
11. They walk at different speeds.
12. Check students' work.
13. the student whose graph has a steeper slope
14–15. Check students' work.
16. The slopes should be about the same because they walked at the same speed.
17. They have the same slope.
18. m
19. The difference is constant because they are walking at the same speed.
20. They are the same line.

Coming and Going   Activity 4

1. No, a motion detector is like a function machine because there is only one distance for any given time.
2. Students should sketch a line of positive slope with a y–intercept near zero. They should also sketch a line of negative slope with a y-intercept near the top of the screen. The negative slope indicates a person walking toward the detector. The positive slope indicates a person walking away from the detector. The y–intercepts show how far from the detectors each person started.
3. Not necessarily. It can be approximated from the data, however.
4–7. Check students' work.
8. Check students' work. If an equation models the data well, the line should overlap the plot. If an equation does not model the data well, the line may either have a different slope or an incorrect y–intercept.
9–10. Check students' work.
11. The measurements should agree closely with the calculations. Discrepancies might be caused by delays due to the reaction times of the marker and timer.
12. A motion detector records only the distance to the closest object in front of it. A motion detector cannot record two objects at once. A function has only one y–value for each x–value.
13. Check students' work.

Keep Your Eye on the Ball   Activity 5

1. The student should sketch a series of parabolas opening downward with maximum values that gradually decrease.
2. decrease
3. Yes, each rebound is shorter than the previous bounce.
4–5. Check students' work.

Answers (continued)

6. vary
7. decreasing
8. Multiply a height value by 75% or 80% and see if the result is the height of the previous bounce.
9. yes; constant
10. Check students' work.
11. $b = -2ax$; check students' work.
12–16. Check students' work.

Race Cars   Activity 6

1. Yes; the battery-powered car gives a linear graph because it travels at a constant speed. The speed of the wind-up car changes, so its graph will show a curve as it speeds up and a curve as it slows down.
2. Students should sketch a line for the battery-powered car and a curve showing the acceleration and deceleration of the wind-up car.
3. The battery-powered car can be modeled by a line. The wind-up car can be modeled by two parabolas, one for acceleration and one for deceleration.
4. Check students' work; a line
5. Check students' work; the slope is the speed and the y–intercept is the initial distance from the motion detector.
6. Check students' work. The equations may not model the data after the car initially starts driving because there is some acceleration.
7. Check students' work.
8. The values should be very close. The slope might be higher than the average speed from the graph because the slope ignores the brief acceleration of the car.
9. $0 < x \leq 1.5$; students may want the domain to extend beyond $x = 1.5$ because the car continues to drive. Any domain that they can justify is reasonable, but it should not be very long, since the car may stop.
10. The collected data would span a longer period of time. Everything else should remain constant.
11. Check students' work. Should be approximately the same as the previous model.
12. Check students' work; yes.
13. $0 \leq x \leq 6$
14. Check students' work.
15. The data will appear linear but you would expect some type of curve. You will see a line because you are recording data for a very short time. But the spring-loaded car must be either speeding up or slowing down since it does not go at a constant speed as does the battery-powered car. Thus you would expect to see a curve.
16. A longer time interval will give a better look at the car's motion. You will probably see s-shaped data. You will see a parabola opening upward for when the car starts and is speeding up and a parabola opening downward for when it is slowing at the end.

Back and Forth It Goes   Activity 7

1. Sketch should resemble a cosine curve with negative amplitude.
2. decrease; increase
3. Check students' work.
4. Students should label the minimums and maximums of the graph. The motion detector records points at regular intervals. It probably does not record the actual minimum and maximum but records points near the maximum and minimum.
5–9. Check students' work.
10. Check students' work; yes; non-linear
11. $y = g\left(\dfrac{x}{2\pi}\right)^2$; check students' work; it should be a good model.
12. 1.74; the two methods should give close answers but there will be some experimental discrepancy.
13. $l = 0.64$; the answer is reasonable, although it does not agree exactly with the measurement from the activity.
14. $t = 2\pi\sqrt{\dfrac{l}{g}}$; independent; as you change the length of the pendulum, the period changes.
15. Check students' work. The model gives $T = 2.84$ s. The model and the experiment should give similar answers.
16. You should shorten it.

Charge It!   Activity 8

1. $f(x); g(x)$
2. a is the starting amount or the y–intercept. b is the base, the growth factor, or the decay factor.
3. $b > 1; 0 < b < 1$
4. $1; 2; y = 2^x$
5. $30; 0.75; y = 30(0.75)^x$
6–7. Check students' work.
8. Check students' work; it is the voltage of the battery.
9. The two answers should be close. The y–intercept may be lower because the capacitor may still have been collecting charge.
10. They are the same.
11. exponential decay
12–15. Check students' work.
16. They should be very close.
17. No, exponential functions never reach their asymptotes. No, the voltage of the capacitor will eventually reach zero.
18. 0.9782; they should be close.

Falling Objects   Activity 9

1. Students should graph a horizontal line with a positive y–intercept that changes to the right side of a downward-opening parabola. There should be a horizontal line once the parabola reaches the x–axis.

Answers (continued)

2. quadratic
3. Check students' work. First the book was held over the motion detector. Next it fell. Finally it lies on top of the motion detector.
4–11. Check students' work.
12. The vertex represents the time at which the student dropped the book and the book's initial height above the motion detector.
13. Check students' work. Only the part of the parabola that corresponds to the actual time the book was falling should be included in the domain. At the other times, the book was actually stationary.
14. Check students' work.
15. The model should not agree exactly. The physics model assumes that there is no air resistance. The book is affected by air resistance. The physics model assumes that the book starts to fall when $t = 0$. In the activity, the book was held briefly so that it started to fall after $t = 0$.

Bouncing Ball, Part 1   Activity 10

1. The student should sketch a series of parabolas that open upward that all stop about 5 units above the x–axis.
2. The student should sketch a series of parabolas opening downward with maximum values that gradually decrease. Students who understand that the motion detector measures distance from itself should understand that the final result will be a graph of the distance from the floor instead of the distance from the motion detector.
3. The ball will bounce to a maximum height that is a percent of the previous height. The percent should be constant.
4–5. Check students' work.
6. One method is to substitute the coordinates of the vertex for h and k; next substitute the coordinates of a point on the parabola for x and y; then solve for a. Another method is to find three points on the parabola and substitute their coordinates into the equation $y = ax^2 + bx + c$; then solve for a, b, and c.
7. Check students' work. The curve is too wide and opens up instead of down.
8. A parabola with a negative a opens down. A parabola with a positive a opens up; negative
9. The curve is narrower. A larger a means a narrower curve. A smaller a means a wider curve.
10. Check students' work, but a should be near -16.
11. No; if students use an actual data point, their models may be off in height or not centered on the bounce horizontally.
12. Check students' work. They should be similar.
13. a is the acceleration due to gravity, h is the time when the ball is at the maximum height, k is the maximum height of the ball for the bounce. a should remain constant because gravity is constant.

Bouncing Ball, Part 2   Activity 11

1. The student should sketch a series of parabolas opening downward with maximum values that gradually decrease.
2. eventually comes to a stop
3. decrease
4. remains constant
5–8. Check students' work.
9. exponential or possibly quadratic
10. A quadratic equation does not have an asymptote. After an infinite amount of time, a quadratic equation predicts that the ball is an infinite distance below the floor. After the same amount of time, an exponential equation predicts that the ball is at 0 ft, or resting on the floor.
11–13. Check students' work.
14. Check students' work. A well-fitting model should approximately touch the vertex of each bounce.
15–16. Check students' work.
17. coefficient of restitution

When's the Tea Ready?   Activity 12

1. 100°C; room temperature. A liquid cannot cool below room temperature.
2. Students should draw an exponential function with an asymptote at room temperature.
3. The graphs will be similar, but the probe should cool more quickly because it has less mass.
4–5. Check students' work.
6. exponential
7. the x–axis
8. Check students' work; no.
9. By adding a constant c, the graph of the exponential equation is translated vertically and the asymptote is no longer the x–axis.
10. c should be given the value found in Exercise 8; it is the temperature of the classroom.
11–13. Check students' work.
14. Check students' work. The model should fit well because it overlaps most of the data points. The model may not fit the first few points.
15. Check students' work.
16. No, a is the difference between the initial value and the room temperature, c.
17. Check students' work. This model is a vertical translation of the previous model. The translation is necessary because the room temperature is greater than zero.
18. yes; yes
19. yes; yes
20–21. Check students' work.
22. a is the difference between room temperature and the initial temperature of the water. b is the rate at which the water cools; it does not change, c is room temperature; it does not change. Check students' work.

Answers (continued)

Full Speed Ahead   Activity 13

1. Students' should sketch a line.
2. Students should sketch a curve opening upward.
3. Students should sketch a curve opening downward.
4. Check students' work; yes.
5. Check students' work; the slope is the speed and the y–intercept is the initial distance from the motion detector.
6. The model should fit reasonably well, the residual plot should show a definite parabolic pattern.
7. quadratic because the speed is increasing
8. Check students' work.
9. The model should fit better. The residuals should confirm the quality of the model.
10. The speed is increasing because as x increases the change in y divided by the change in x is getting larger. This means that the car is traveling farther during each x-unit.
11. The sketch should show a parabola opening upward representing an increase in speed joined to a parabola opening downward. The data shows the car speeding up at the start and then slowing down.
12. The model is reasonable only over the domain $0 \le x \le 1.5$. The time interval was too short to see the car slow down.
13. Check students' work. Students should label when the car is accelerating and decelerating.
14–15. Check students' work. Models should fit well.
16. Students can use the **intersect** option on the graphing calculator or solve the system of quadratic equations formed by the two models. Check students' work.

In the Swing of Things   Activity 14

1. The graph should be a periodic function with a maximum or minimum at the y–axis.
2. the length of the string
3. cosine or sine
4. a = amplitude; $b = 2\pi$ divided by the period; c = horizontal translation; d = vertical translation
5–7. Check students' work.
8. Take half the difference between the y–value of a peak and the y–value of a trough. Check students' work.
9. Take the difference between the x–values of two peaks or two trough. Check students' work.
10. Find the x–value of the first peak. Check students' work.
11. Take the average of the y–values of one peak and one trough. Check students' work.
12–13. Check students' work.
14. The amplitude is greater, because the pendulum is pulled back farther. The graph has a greater vertical translation because the motion detector sill needs to be 1.5 m away from the closest swing of the pendulum.
15. The period decreases because the string is longer. The amplitude and vertical translation increase because a longer string means that the pendulum starts farther away from the center of its swing.

16. The magnitude of a is determined by the angle at which the string is pulled back and by the length of the string. b decreases with the length of the string. c increases when the motion detector is started after the pendulum is swinging. d increases when the string is pulled back farther and when the string is longer.

Playing With Numbers   Activity 15

Investigate

1. See screen
2. The digits are the same but in a different order.
3. The digits are the same but in a different order.

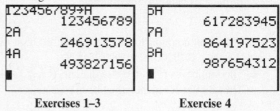

Exercises 1–3   Exercise 4

4. Yes
5. Same digits with zero included

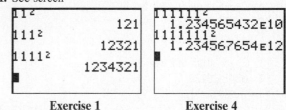

Exercise 5

6. Multiples of 3 have been omitted from the list.
7. 22A, 23A, 25A, 26A
8. The same patterns occur.

Investigate

1. See screen

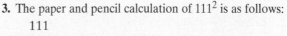

Exercise 1   Exercise 4

2. $11111^2 = 123454321$
3. The paper and pencil calculation of 111^2 is as follows:

$$\begin{array}{r} 111 \\ \times 111 \\ \hline 111 \\ 111 \\ 111 \\ \hline 12321 \end{array}$$

Notice that the number of one's in each column increases (then decreases) by 1 from right to left.
4. It can be seen that the digits increase (then decrease) by 1 from left to right.
5. The last 7 in the number has been rounded up from 6.

Answers (continued)

6. Using paper and pencil, it can be seen that there is a column of 10 one's, whose sum is 10. This results in a "carry-over" which causes the pattern to break down.

Investigate

1. Answers may vary. Sample: 82471
2. Answers may vary. Sample: 27814
3. Answers may vary. Sample: $82471 - 27814 = 54657$
4. Answers may vary. Sample:
   $5 + 4 + 6 + 5 + 7 = 27; 72 - 27 = 45;$
   $4 + 5 = 9$
5. A sum of 9 always results.
6. Variables can take on any numerical value, therefore proving a result for any number.

Exercises

1. The result contains five copies of the two-digit number (i.e. $48 \cdot 101010101 = 4848484848$).
2. The number is repeated as a decimal (i.e. $\frac{4}{9} = .\overline{4}$). They do not terminate; they keep repeating.
3. Yes. In this case $\frac{9}{9} = 1$ and $.\overline{9} = 1$ as well.
4. The number is repeated as a decimal (i.e. $\frac{36}{99} = .\overline{36}$).
5. Yes. In this case $\frac{99}{99} = 1$ and $.\overline{99} = 1$ as well.

Finding Real Roots of Equations   Activity 16

Investigate

1–3. Check student's work.
4. .8241323123
5. −.8241323123

Investigate

6. Check student's work.
7. −.8241323123

Investigate

1. Check student's work.
2. .8241323123
3. −.8241323123

Exercises

1. They are approximations.
2. .3862368706; 1.961569035
3. The (x, y) coordinates of the graphs are real numbers, so graphical methods can only reveal real answers.

Solving Absolute Value Inequalities Graphically   Activity 17

Investigate

1–3. Check student's work.

Investigate

4. Check student's work.
5. All values of x where the graph is below the x-axis.

6. All values of x where the graph is on or above the x-axis.

Investigate

7. Check student's work.
8. The inequality returns a value of -1 for $1 \le x \le 3$ and 0 everywhere else. The points on the graph with y-coordinate 0 are hidden by the x-axis.

Exercises

1. $-2 \le x \le 1$; methods of solution may vary
2. $-\frac{1}{7} < x < \frac{5}{7}$
3. $\frac{4}{3} < x < 3$
4. $1 < x < 2$

Magic Pricing Numbers   Activity 18

Investigate

1. $\frac{1}{24}$ or 24^{-1}
2. 1.16
3. .9
4. 1.028
5. $\frac{1}{24} \cdot 1.16 \cdot .9 \cdot 1.028 = .044718$
6. $y = .044718x$
7. Here are two examples to describe the rounding process. The number 31.243 typically rounds down to 31.24 (to the nearest penny). By adding .005, you get $31.243 + .005 = 31.248$ which rounds up to 31.25. The number 31.247 typically rounds up to 31.25. By adding .005, you get $31.247 + .005 = 31.252$ which still rounds to 31.25.
8. Yes
9. $28.81

Exercises

1. $21.62
2. Multiply 857.98 by $\frac{1}{36} \cdot 1.16 \cdot .9 \cdot 1.028 = .029812$; $y = .029812(857.98) = \$25.58$
3. $w = (.044718)^{-1} = 22.36236x$, where $w =$ wholesale price and $x =$ retail price

Mrs. Murphy's Algebra Test Scores   Activity 19

Investigate

1. first line: 30 units; second line: 20 units
2. $x - 42$
3. $\frac{x - 42}{30}$
4. $y - 78; \frac{y - 78}{20}$
5. $\frac{x - 42}{30} = \frac{y - 78}{20}$
6. The graph is a straight line.

Exercises

1. 60

Answers (continued)

2. $\dfrac{x - 32}{40} = \dfrac{y - 78}{20}$ or $y = \dfrac{1}{2}(x - 32) + 78$

3. $\dfrac{x - 40}{36} = \dfrac{y - 72}{27}$ or $y = \dfrac{3}{4}(x - 40) + 72$

Exploring Point-Slope Form   Activity 20

Investigate
1. $y - 1 = 3(x - 2)$
2–4. Check student's work.
5. $L3 = \{-2, -1, -.5, 0, .5, 1, 2\}$

Exercises

1.
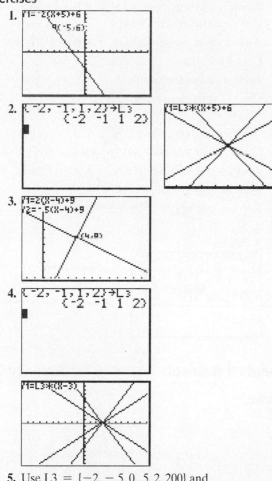

2. $\{-2, -1, 1, 2\} \to L3$
   $\{-2 \ \ -1 \ \ 1 \ \ 2\}$

3.

4. $\{-2, -1, 1, 2\} \to L3$
   $\{-2 \ \ -1 \ \ 1 \ \ 2\}$

5. Use $L3 = \{-2, -.5, 0, .5, 2, 200\}$ and
   $Y1 = L3 * (X - 12) + 12$

Fast Food Follies   Activity 21

Investigate
1. $3x + 4y + 4z = 16.45$
   $5x + 2y + 5z = 19.30$
   $4x + 6y + 6z = 23.50$
2. The product of matrix A and matrix X will produce matrix B.
3. If $AX = B$, then $X = A^{-1}B$.

4–6. Check student's work.

Exercises

1.
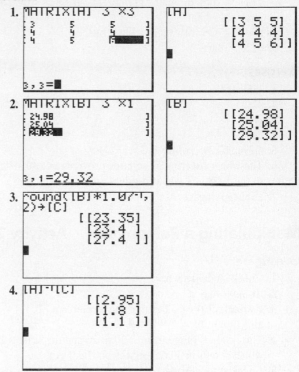

2.

3.

4.

Burgers cost $2.95; Fries cost $1.80; Soft Drinks cost $1.10

5. If it costs $25.04 for 4 burgers, 4 fries, and 4 soft drinks, then it should cost $25.04 \div 2 = \$12.52$ for 2 burgers, 2 fries, and 2 soft drinks. The screen at right shows the error message that results when $[A]^{-1}[C]$ is executed.

Wheat on a Chessboard   Activity 22

Investigate

1.	Square	Num. of Grains	2.	Num. of Squares	Total Num. of Grains
	1	1		1	1
	2	2		2	3
	3	4		3	7
	4	8		4	15
	5	16		5	31
	6	32		6	63
	7	64		7	127
	8	128		8	255
	9	256		9	511
	10	512		10	1023

Answers (continued)

3. Raise 2 to the number of squares and subtract 1.
4. $T(n) = 2^n - 1$ where n = number of squares and
   $T(n)$ = total number of grains; about 1.8×10^{19}
   grains of wheat
5. about 1.7×10^{13} or 17 trillion bushels
6. 6728.3 years

Exercises

1. 1,075,000
2. 21
3. 20
4. 255
5. 4,294,967,295 (which is $2^{32} - 1$)
6. The wheat covering 51 squares provides a close match
   to the 1998 U.S. wheat production.
7. about 2.6 inches

Manipulating a Polynomial   Activity 23

Investigate

1. Check student's work.
2. It moves up.
3. Evaluate $f(0) = 12$ to find the y-intercept, $(0, 12)$,
   and $12 > 10$.
4. The y-values range from -20 to 20 and the scale is 1,
   which results in 40 tick marks on the y-axis.
5. Check student's work.

Investigate

1. Because the polynomial has a value of 0 when $x = -1$.
2. Check student's work.
3–4. Answers may vary. Sample:
   $f(x) = (5x^4 - 17x^3 + 13x^2 - 8x + 12)(x + 1)(x + 3)$;
   graph shown with $Xmin = -4.7, Xmax = 4.7$,
   $Xscl = 1, Ymin = -440, Ymax = 100, Yscl = 0$

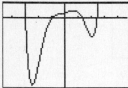

Exercises

1. Answers may vary. Sample:
   $f(x) = (x + 3)(x - 1)(x - 3)(x - 5)$; graph shown
   with $Xmin = -4.7, Xmax = 6, Xscl = 1$,
   $Ymin = -120, Ymax = 20, Yscl = 0$

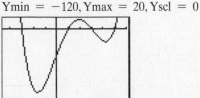

2. No portion of the graph can be seen in the ZDecimal
   window.

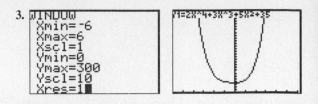

Writing a Simple Program   Activity 24

Investigate

1–8. Check student's work.

Exercises

1. Answers may vary. Sample: $A = 1, B = 1$, and
   $C = -20$ has roots -5 and 4.
2. Answers may vary. Sample: $A = 4, B = -12$, and
   $C = 9$ has root $\frac{3}{2}$.
3. Answers may vary. Sample: $A = 2, B = -5$, and
   $C = 7$ has imaginary roots $\frac{5}{4} - 1.392i$ and $\frac{5}{4} + 1.392i$.

4. Answers may vary. Sample: $A = 6, B = 7$, and
   $C = -5$ has rational roots $-\frac{5}{3}$ and $\frac{1}{2}$.
5. Answers may vary. Sample: $A = 3, B = 8$, and
   $C = -7$ has irrational roots $\frac{-4 \pm \sqrt{37}}{3}$
   (-3.361 and $.694$).
6. a. $625.72
   b. $2236.58

```
PROGRAM:BALANCE
:Fix 2
:Prompt P,R,N,T
:Disp "BALANCE:
",P(1+R/N)^(N*T)
:Float
```

Repeated Radicals   Activity 25

Exercises

1. 9
2.
$$x = 6 + \sqrt{6 + \sqrt{6 + \sqrt{6 + \sqrt{6 + \ldots}}}}$$
$$(x - 6)^2 = \left(\sqrt{6 + \sqrt{6 + \sqrt{6 + \sqrt{6 + \ldots}}}}\right)^2$$
$$x^2 - 12x + 36 = 6 + \sqrt{6 + \sqrt{6 + \sqrt{6 + \ldots}}}$$
$$x^2 - 12x + 36 = x$$
$$x^2 - 13x + 36 = 0$$
$$(x - 4)(x - 9) = 0$$
$$x = 4 \text{ and } x = 9$$
The solution $x = 4$ is extraneous, since x is clearly
greater than 6.
3. 5.302775638; the number is an approximation
4. $\frac{7 + \sqrt{13}}{2}$; irrational
5. The calculator can only give an approximate answer,
   whereas algebraic techniques give an exact answer.

Answers (continued)

Asymptotes and Holes   Activity 26

Investigate

1. The function is undefined at $x = \pm 2$. This makes sense algebraically since the denominator is equal to zero at these two values of x.
2. It disappears.
3. The function approaches $\pm\infty$ on either side of the singularity. This makes sense because the denominator approaches zero as x approaches the singularity.
4. Vertical lines appear at the singularities.
5. The y–value 'jumps' from negative to positive (or vice versa) as you trace through a singularity.
6. The calculator was drawing a line between two points on either side of the singularity.
7. Yes; the singularity at $x = -2$ appears as a hole in the graph.
8. The function is undefined when the denominator is equal to zero.
9. As you approach the singularity at $x = -2$ from the left or right, the corresponding y–values approach the same number. As you approach the singularity at $x = 2$ from the left, the y–values approach $-\infty$. As you approach the singularity at $x = 2$ from the right, the y–values approach $+\infty$.
10. No; the simplified function is defined at $x = -2$ and the hole disappears.
11. When graphing Y1, the graphing ball 'breaks' when it reaches $x = -2$. This does not happen when you graph Y2.

Exercises

1. The first graph has a hole at $x = 1$ whereas the second graph does not. The domain of $y = \dfrac{x^2 - 1}{x - 1}$ is all real numbers except 1 and the domain of $y = x + 1$ is all real numbers.
2. Answers may vary. Sample: $f(x) = \dfrac{2}{(x + 1)(x - 1)}$
3. Answers may vary. Sample: $f(x) = \dfrac{x^3 - x^2}{x - 1}$ or $f(x) = \dfrac{x^2(x - 1)}{x - 1}$
4. Check student's work.
5. Type '.05 $\to \triangle$X' on the home screen to eliminate false asymptotes.

Stepping Out   Activity 27

Investigate

1. The graph resembles a series of steps.
2. The range values are $\{1, 2, 4, 3, 4\}$. Answers may vary. Sample: 'Int' rounds numbers down to the nearest integer.
3. The range values are $\{-2, -2, -5, -4, -5\}$. Answers may vary. Sample: 'Int' rounds numbers to the nearest integer that is less than or equal to the number.

4. The calculator will connect the endpoints of each step to the next step.
5.

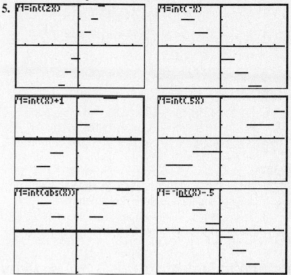

6. 6; 11; the function $C(x) = 3.50 + 2.50x$ models a cost that varies continuously as a function of mileage, whereas the actual cost increases in steps.
7. The function rounds the mileage *down*, whereas the cab company rounds the mileage *up*. For example, a 4.4 mile trip is charged at the same rate as a 4 mile trip instead of a 5 mile trip.
8. $C(x) = 3.50 + 2.50\text{int}(x + 1)$

Exercises

1. $C(x) = .34 + .23\text{int}(x + 1)$
2. The two functions are identical except at the integer values. A careful graph of $y = \text{int}(x + 1)$ would show a closed dot on the left of each step and an open dot on the right, while a careful graph of $y = -\text{int}(-x)$ would show an open dot on the left of each step and a closed dot on the right.
3. Answers may vary. Sample: Y1 $= 3.5 - 2.5\text{int}(-x)$; Answers may vary. Sample: Y1 $= .34 - .23\text{int}(-x)$

Systems With Many Solutions   Activity 28

Investigate

1. The error message 'ERR:SINGULAR MAT' appears.
2. Yes
3. $2x + 3y + z = 6.85$
   $4x + 3y + 3z = 11.65$
   $3x + 3y + 2z = 9.25$;
   Yes; the prices given in the previous question solve the system.
4. Because matrix A does not have an inverse.
5. 6.85; 11.65; 9.25
6. 6.85; 11.65; 9.25
7. There can only be one matrix $[A]^{-1}[B]$, so the calculator could not produce multiple correct answers in this way.

Answers (continued)

Exercises

1. Check students' work.
2. Any values of $x, y,$ and z satisfy the equation.
3. $3\left(y - \frac{1}{3}z\right) = 3\left(\frac{41}{60}\right) \rightarrow 3y - z = \frac{41}{20} \rightarrow$
   $3y - z = 2.05$
4. $x + z = \frac{12}{5}$
5. $x = 2.2; z = .2$
6. $2(2.2) + 3(.75) + 2 = 6.85 \rightarrow 6.85 = 6.85$
   $4(2.2) + 3(.75) + 3(2) = 11.65 \rightarrow 11.65 = 11.65$
   $3(2.2) + 3(.75) + 2(2) = 9.25 \rightarrow 9.25 = 9.25$

Extend

7. the cost of a burger is too low; some of the numbers are not rounded to the nearest penny.
8. Answers may vary. Sample: $1.30, $1.05, $1.10; $1.60, $0.95, $0.80; $1.90, $0.85, $0.50

Parabolic Reflectors   Activity 29

Investigate

1–4. Check students' work.
5. They are equal.
6. Check students' work.

Exercises

1. $(0, 4)$
2. closer
3. By placing the lamp at the focus of a parabolic reflector, all rays that strike the reflector are directed outward parallel to the axis. This helps 'concentrate' the light in a specific direction.

Exploring Powers of –1   Activity 30

Investigate

1. Check students' work.
2. $(-1)^{\frac{2}{6}} = -1; [(-1)^2]^{\frac{1}{6}} = 1;$ The calculator evaluates $(-1)^{\frac{2}{6}}$ as $(-1)^{\frac{1}{3}} = -1,$ whereas the law of exponents would seem to imply that $(-1)^{\frac{2}{6}} = [(-1)^2]^{\frac{1}{6}} = 1^{\frac{1}{6}} = 1.$ The answer depends on the fraction being reduced to lowest terms before the laws of exponents are applied.
3. It reduces $\frac{2}{6}$ to $\frac{1}{3},$ which is the same as taking the cube root.
4. Values of x are considered as fractions in lowest terms before being used as exponents. For example, $f(.4)$ is evaluated as $f\left(\frac{2}{5}\right) = (-1)^{\frac{2}{5}} = 1. f(.5)$ is evaluated as $f\left(\frac{1}{2}\right) = (-1)^{\frac{1}{2}}$ which is undefined and $f(.6)$ is evaluated as $f\left(\frac{3}{5}\right) = (-1)^{\frac{3}{5}} = -1.$
5. Using this window, the calculator attempts (but fails) to evaluate $y = (-1)^x$ for values of x that are irra-

tional. This explains why no graph results.
6. The calculator only evaluates $y = (-1)^x$ for values of x that only have real answers (such as $x = \frac{2}{5}, \frac{3}{5}, \frac{4}{5}, \dots$). These values cause y to alternate between -1 and 1.
7. The calculator only evaluates $y = (-1)^x$ for values of x whose fractions reduce such that the numerators are always even numbers (such as $x = \frac{2}{5}, \frac{4}{5}, \frac{6}{5}, \dots$). These x–values always produce y–values of 1.
8. The calculator only evaluates $y = (-1)^x$ for values of x whose fractions reduce such that the numerators are always odd numbers (such as $x = \frac{1}{5}, \frac{3}{5}, \frac{5}{5}, \dots$). These x–values always produce y–values of $-1.$

Exercises

1. $y = (-2)^x; y = (-2)^{-x}; y = 2(-1)^x$
2. π is irrational—it cannot be written as the quotient of two integers; use a rational approximation for π such as $\frac{314159}{100000}.$

Bull's-eyes   Activity 31

Investigate

1. Check students' work.
2. Check students' work.
3.

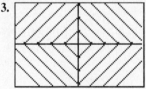

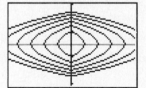

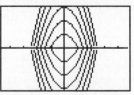

4. the second and third one
5. type the function shown below

Answers (continued)

Exercises

1. D: $-2 \leq x \leq 2$
R: $0 \leq y \leq 2$

D: $-4 \leq x \leq 4$
R: $0 \leq y \leq 4$

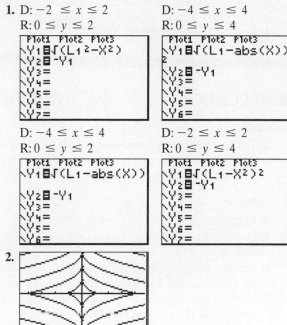

D: $-4 \leq x \leq 4$
R: $0 \leq y \leq 2$

D: $-2 \leq x \leq 2$
R: $0 \leq y \leq 4$

2.

3. Check students' work.

The Natural Logarithm   Activity 32

Investigate

1. Check students' work.
2. 1
3. Check students' work.
4. Upper limit $= e$

Exercises

1. .6931471806; ln(2) $=$ .6931471806; the two numbers are equal
2. they are equal
3. they are equal
4. it is negative
5. For any $a > 0$, $\ln(a) =$ the area under the graph of $y = \frac{1}{x}$ between $x = 1$ and $x = a$, with "area" being negative for $0 < a < 1$.

Can a Graph Cross Its   Activity 33
Own Asymptote?

Investigate

1. The x–axis
2. no
3. yes; $Y2 = \frac{x}{(x^2 + 1)}$
4. twice
5. three times
6. yes

Exercises

1. Answers may vary. Sample: $y = \dfrac{(x^2 - 1)(x^2 - 4)}{x^6 + 1}$
2. The graph crosses its own asymptote an infinite number of times.
3. Yes, because the function gets arbitrarily close to $y = 2$ as x approaches $\pm\infty$. The fact that the function actually *equals* 2 is technically not an issue.
4. Answers may vary. Sample: x^2 if $x \leq 0$

Making Ellipses   Activity 34
out of Circles

Investigate

1–3. Check students' work.
4. It looks identical to the graph shown in the introduction.
5. A horizontal ellipse with major axis of length 6 and minor axis of length 4 is a circle of radius 1 that is stretched horizontally by a factor of 3 and vertically by a factor of 2. These scale factors can be produced by dividing the x–axis window values by 3 and the y–axis window values by 2.

Exercises

1. Divide Xmin, Xmax, and Xscl by 2; divide Ymin, Ymax, and Yscl by 3.

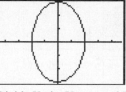

2. Divide Xmin, Xmax, and Xscl by 4; divide Ymin, Ymax, and Yscl by 3.

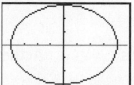

3. Divide the X–Window values by 6 and the Y–Window values by 2. The graph does not fit in the window.

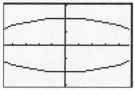

Answers (continued)

Extend

4. First, multiply Xmin, Xmax, Ymin, and Ymax by 2. Then follow the steps in the answer to Exercise #3 above.

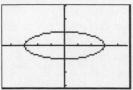

5. First, multiply Xmin, Xmax, Ymin, and Ymax by 2. Then divide Xmin, Xmax, and Xscl by 2 and divide Ymin, Ymax, and Yscl by 6.

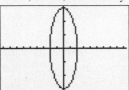

6. First, multiply Xmin, Xmax, Ymin, and Ymax by 2. Then divide Xmin, Xmax, and Xscl by 2 and divide Ymin, Ymax, and Yscl by 6. Finally, add 3/6 to Ymin and Ymax to re-center the screen vertically. The circle command will be 'Circle(2/2, 3/6, 1).'

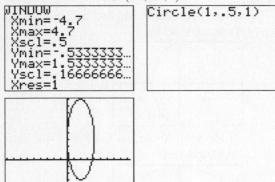

The Harmonic Series $\qquad$ Activity 35

Investigate

1. The graph rises (slowly) without bound.
2. $y = e^x$; all reals
3. $1, \frac{1}{2}, \frac{1}{3}, \ldots ; 1, \frac{1}{2}, \frac{1}{3}, \ldots$
4. In both figures, the area of the rectangles represents the terms of the harmonic sequence. The expression $\ln(a)$ represents the area under the curve from $x = 1$ to $x = a$. Since the rectangles are all above the curve, the inequality $1 + \frac{1}{2} + \frac{1}{3} + \cdots + \frac{1}{a} > \ln(a)$ must be true. In the second inequality, since the rectangles are entirely contained within the region below the curve, the inequality, $1 + \frac{1}{2} + \frac{1}{3} + \cdots + \frac{1}{a} < 1 + \ln(a)$, must be true.
5. between 9.21 and 10.21

Exercises

1. Check students' work.
2. 5.187377518; $\ln(100) \approx 4.605, 1 + \ln(100) \approx 5.605$
3. 6.79282343; $\ln(500) \approx 6.215, 1 + \ln(500) \approx 7.215$
4. No; it's between $\ln(10^9) = 20.723$ and $1 + \ln(10^9) = 21.723$.
5. $e^{100} \approx 2.688 \times 10^{43}$ terms

Monte Carlo π $\qquad$ Activity 36

Investigate

1. The probability that a randomly selected point lies within the shaded region is equal to the ratio of the area of the shaded region to the area of the square, that is, $\frac{\frac{\pi}{4}}{1} = \frac{\pi}{4}$
2. Check students' work.
3. Because the coordinates, A and B, will always be less than or equal to 1.
4. Answers may vary. Sample: The ratio will most likely fall between 2 and 5, with most results clustered near 3.2.
5. Answers may vary. Sample: The ratio should consistently be very close to 3.14.

Exercises

1. Line 1: Clears any drawings
   Line 2: Turns off all plots
   Line 3: Turns off any functions located in the 'Y=' editor
   Line 4: Sets the viewing window, graphs square, graphs circle
   Line 5: Set the value of H equal to 0
   Line 6: Prompts the user to input the number of points for the simulation
   Line 7: Sets up a loop that will execute the next 4 lines N times; K is a counter
   Line 8: Stores random numbers between 0 and 1 as A and B
   Line 9: Plots the ordered pairs (A, B) on the graph
   Line 10: Calculates the distance from the origin to point (A, B) and tests if this distance is less than or equal to 1 (determines if the point is within the circle)
   Line 11: Adds 1 to the value of H if the point falls within the circle.
   Line 12: Specifies where the loop ends, which happens when K is equal to N
   Lines 13 and 14: Displays "4 * RATIO IS:" along with the value of 4H/N (which should be approximately equal to π)
2. Check students' work.

The Way the Ball Bounces $\qquad$ Activity 37

Investigate

1–2. Check students' work.
3. A ball bouncing on a spring.

Answers (continued)

4. The ball moves quicker as it passes through the origin because its motion is mostly in the vertical direction (keeping in mind that that ball is really traveling along a unit circle). The ball moves slower at the top and bottom of its path because its motion is mostly in the horizontal direction.
5. Yes

Exercises

1. The ball moves twice as fast.
2. Change Tmax to 18π.
3. 3 cycles of a sine curve.
4. Nothing; the scale along the x–axis is so large that the graph is entirely contained along the y–axis and cannot be seen.
5. The wave has been compressed horizontally (because of the large x–axis scale), giving a result identical to step 3 of the investigation.
6. The vertical position of a point traveling along a unit circle at a constant speed can be used to model harmonic motion. If the vertical motion is graphed as a function of time, it generates a sine wave.

Graphing Ellipses and Hyperbolas   Activity 38

Investigate

1–2. Check students' work.

3. $\dfrac{x^2}{9} + \dfrac{y^2}{4} = \dfrac{(3\cos T)^2}{9} + \dfrac{(2\sin T)^2}{4} =$
$\dfrac{9\cos^2 T}{9} + \dfrac{4\sin^2 T}{4} = \cos^2 T + \sin^2 T = 1$; horizontal stretch factor $= a$, vertical stretch factor $= b$

4. $x^2 - y^2 = \dfrac{1}{\cos^2 T} - \dfrac{\sin^2 T}{\cos^2 T} = \dfrac{1 - \sin^2 T}{\cos^2 T} =$
$\dfrac{\cos^2 T}{\cos^2 T} = 1$; a hyperbola

5. Check students' work.

Exercises

1. $\tan T$
2. 3; 2
3. $\text{X1T} = \dfrac{3}{\cos T}$; $\text{Y1T} = \dfrac{2\sin T}{\cos T} = 2\tan T$

Vertical Angles   Activity 39

Investigate

1. They are congruent.
2. $m\angle EAD + m\angle EAB = 180$
3. $m\angle EAD + m\angle BAC = 180$
4. $(\angle EAD + \angle EAB) - (\angle EAB + \angle BAC) = 0$
5. $(\angle EAD + \angle EAB) - (\angle EAB + \angle BAC) = 0$ simplifies to $\angle EAD - \angle BAC = 0$ which means $\angle EAD = \angle BAC$

Extend

6. Check students' work.
7. They are perpendicular.
8. Answers may vary. Sample: Adjacent angles are supplementary. The angle bisectors of these angles create a pair of angles that are complementary.

Exterior Angles of Triangles   Activity 40

Investigate

1. The measure of an exterior angle of a triangle is equal to the sum of the remote interior angles.
2. supplementary; $\angle A + \angle B + \angle ACB = 180$ and $\angle ACB + \angle BCD = 180$; rewrite both equations as $\angle A + \angle B = 180 - \angle ACB$ and $\angle BCD = 180 - \angle ACB$; by substitution $\angle A + \angle B = \angle BCD$

Extend

3. their sum is 90; they must be complementary since the angles of a triangle have a sum of 90 and $\angle B = 90$
4. their sum is 270;
$\angle DAC + \angle ACE = (\angle BAC + \angle B) + (\angle ACB + \angle B) = (\angle BAC + \angle ACB) + (\angle B + \angle B) = 90 + 180 = 270$

Investigate Further

5. $\angle ADE - (\angle A + \angle B + \angle C) = 180$;
$\angle ADE + 180 = \angle A + \angle B + \angle C$;
$\angle A + \angle B + \angle C + \angle ADC = 360$ and $\angle ADC + \angle ADE = 180$;
$\angle A + \angle B + \angle C = 360 - \angle ADC$ and $\angle ADE = 180 - \angle ADC$; by substitution $\angle ADE + 180 = \angle A + \angle B + \angle C$
6. the sum of the remote interior angles of a pentagon is equal to the sum of the exterior angle and 360.
7. Answers may vary. Sample:

No. of Sides	Ext. $\angle$	Sum of Remote Int. $\triangle$	Ext. $\angle -$ Sum of Remote Int. $\triangle$
3	80	80	0
4	80	260	180
5	80	440	360
6	80	620	540

The sum of the remote interior angles of any convex polygon is equal to $E + (n - 3)180$ where E is the measure of the exterior angle and n is the number of sides of the polygon.

Relationships in Triangles   Activity 41

Investigate

1. They are congruent.
2. The triangles are congruent by SAS.
3. $\overline{BE} \cong \overline{AD}$ by CPCTC

Answers (continued)

Extend

4. They are congruent.
5. $\triangle FAC \cong \triangle BAE$ by SAS so $\overline{CF} \cong \overline{BE}$ by CPCTC

Investigate Further

6. they are equal to 120
7. Each angle of the triangle must be less than 120.
8. yes
9. It is equal to the sum of the lengths of the two shortest sides of the triangle.

Isosceles Triangles   Activity 42

Investigate

1. isosceles
2. $\angle DBC$ and $\angle DCB$ are congruent therefore $\triangle BCD$ remains isosceles
3. $\overleftrightarrow{AD}$ is the perpendicular bisector of $\overline{BC}$

Investigate

4. The area of $\triangle ABC$ is twice the area of $ADFE$.
5. the height is half that of $\triangle ABC$.
6. $DE = \frac{1}{2}BC$.
7. Each of the smaller triangles, $\triangle ADE$ and $\triangle DEF$, have base and height that are half those of $\triangle ABC$. Therefore, the areas of each smaller triangle is $\frac{1}{2} \cdot \frac{1}{2} = \frac{1}{4} \triangle ABC$. Together, the areas of $\triangle ADE$ and $\triangle DEF$ must be half the area of $\triangle ABC$.
8. They have the same area.
9. The slopes of $\triangle DEF$ are equal to the corresponding slopes of $\triangle ABC$. The measures of the sides of $\triangle DEF$ are one-half the measure of the corresponding sides of $\triangle ABC$. This is a demonstration of the *midsegment theorem*.
10. yes

Orthocenters   Activity 43

Investigate

1. **a.** when the triangle is acute;
   b. when the triangle is right;
   c. when the triangle is obtuse
2. the orthocenter of $\triangle ABD$ is C; the orthocenter of $\triangle BCD$ is A; the orthocenter of $\triangle ACD$ is B

Investigate

3. The circumferences and areas of all four circles are equal.

Quadrilaterals   Activity 44

Investigate

1. parallelogram
2. They are equal; They are parallel to $\overline{BD}$.
3. One pair of opposite sides of $EHGF$ are congruent and parallel.

4. parallelogram
5. rectangle
6. The diagonals of a rhombus are perpendicular, therefore the sides of $EHGF$ are perpendicular.
7. rhombus
8. square
9. rhombus
10. rectangle
11. If a quadrilateral has congruent diagonals, then the figure formed by joining consecutive midpoints is a rhombus.
12. If a quadrilateral has perpendicular diagonals, then the figure formed by joining consecutive midpoints is a rectangle.
13. Opposite sides of a kite are not parallel. Both pairs of opposite sides of an isosceles trapezoid are not parallel.

Using Different Menus to   Activity 45
Construct Special
Quadrilaterals

Investigate

1–2. kite; two pairs of congruent, adjacent sides

Investigate Further

3. rectangle
4. Check students' work.
5. rhombus
6. rhombus

Extend

rectangle; congruent diagonals bisect each other

Parallelograms and   Activity 46
Triangles

Investigate

1. Check students' work.
2. $\angle BAD$ is twice $\angle AFD$; $\angle ABC$ is twice $\angle BEC$
3. $\angle BAD = \angle AFD + \angle ADF$ by the Exterior Angle Theorem; $\angle AFD \cong \angle ADF$ by the 3. Isosceles Triangle Theorem; therefore, by substitution, $\angle BAD = 2\angle AFD$ or $\frac{1}{2}\angle BAD = \angle AFD$; same reasoning used to show $\frac{1}{2}\angle ABC = \angle BEC$
4. $\angle BEC + \angle AFD = 90$, therefore $\angle CHD = 90$
5. $\angle HCD \cong \angle BEC$ and $\angle CDH \cong \angle AFD$
6. Corresponding Angles Postulate

Regular Polygons   Activity 47

Investigate

1. rhombus
2. 108
3. isosceles
4. 36

Answers (continued)

5. $m\angle GDE = m\angle GFE = 72; m\angle E = 108$

6. 108, since the measures of a quadrilateral have a sum of 360

7. $\overline{DE} \cong \overline{EF}$

8. Since opposite angles are congruent, *DGFE* is a parallelogram. Because a pair of adjacent sides is congruent, *DGFE* is a rhombus.

Extend

9. rhombus

10. Check students' work.

11. Check students' work.

12. Draw the first diagonal such that it is parallel to one of the sides of the regular polygon. The second diagonal will join vertices that are adjacent to the first diagonal such that the diagonals intersect.

Area   Activity 48

Investigate

1. both ratios are 2:1

2. the area of *ABCD* is $3x \cdot 3x = 9x^2$; the area of $\triangle ABF = \text{area } \triangle ADF = \frac{1}{2} \cdot 2x \cdot 3x = 3x^2$; the area of $AECF = 9x^2 - 3x^2 - 3x^2 = 3x^2$; the areas are equal

3. Check students' work.

4. *E* and *G* are midpoints of $\overline{BC}$ and $\overline{CD}$, respectively; *F* coincides with *C*

5. Using *x* to represent the length of one side of *ABCD*, each triangle has measure $\frac{1}{2} \cdot x \cdot 2x = x^2$. The areas are equal.

6. The sides to which the segments are drawn are divided into segments in a ratio of 2:2:1.

7. The sides to which the segments are drawn are divided into segments in a ratio of 1:1:1.

8. The sides to which the segments are drawn are divided into equal segments.

9. The sides to which the segments are drawn are divided into segments in a ratio of 2:2:. . . :2:1.

Pythagorean Triples   Activity 49

Investigate

1. Plato's method uses the formulas

n	$\dfrac{n^2}{4} - 1$	n	$\dfrac{n^2}{4} + 1$
4	$= A2 \cdot A2/4 - 1$	$= A2$	$= A2 \cdot A2/4 + 1$
$= A2 + 2$	$= A3 \cdot A3/4 - 1$	$= A3$	$= A3 \cdot A3/4 + 1$
$= A3 + 2$	$= A4 \cdot A4/4 - 1$	$= A4$	$= A4 \cdot A4/4 + 1$

which produces the following triples

n	$\dfrac{n^2}{4} - 1$	n	$\dfrac{n^2}{4} + 1$
4	3	4	5
6	8	6	10

2. Pythagoras' method uses the formulas

n	$\dfrac{(n^2 - 1)}{2}$	n	$\dfrac{(n^2 + 1)}{2}$
3	$= (A2 \cdot A2 - 1)/2$	$= A2$	$= (A2 \cdot A2 + 1)/2$
$= A2 + 2$	$= (A3 \cdot A3 - 1)/2$	$= A3$	$= (A3 \cdot A3 + 1)/2$
$= A3 + 2$	$= (A4 \cdot A4 - 1)/2$	$= A4$	$= (A4 \cdot A4 + 1)/2$

which produces the following triples

n	$\dfrac{(n^2 - 1)}{2}$	n	$\dfrac{(n^2 + 1)}{2}$
3	4	3	5
5	12	5	13
7	24	7	25

3. The formulas

n	$2n + 1$	$2n^2 + 2n$	$2n^2 + 2n + 1$
1	$= 2 \cdot A2 + 1$	$= 2 \cdot A2 \cdot A2 + 2 \cdot A2$	$= 2 \cdot A2 \cdot A2 + 2 \cdot A2 + 1$
$= A2 + 1$	$= 2 \cdot A3 + 1$	$= 2 \cdot A3 \cdot A3 + 2 \cdot A3$	$= 2 \cdot A3 \cdot A3 + 2 \cdot A3 + 1$
$= A3 + 1$	$= 2 \cdot A4 + 1$	$= 2 \cdot A4 \cdot A4 + 2 \cdot A4$	$= 2 \cdot A4 \cdot A4 + 2 \cdot A4 + 1$

produce the following triples

n	$2n + 1$	$2n^2 + 2n$	$2n^2 + 2n + 1$
1	3	4	5
2	5	12	13
3	7	24	25

4. Plato's method and Pythagoras' method generate triples from the same 'family' of integers, but not necessarily the exact same numbers. For example, the Pythagoras method produces the triple 5, 12, 13 whereas Plato's method produces 10, 24, 26, which is a multiple of 5, 12, 13. The unattributed method produces the same triples as the Pythagoras method.

Similarity   Activity 50

Investigate

1. parallelogram

2. The sides of *PQRS* are midsegments, and therefore parallel, to the sides of *ABCD*.

3. corresponding angles are congruent; corresponding sides are in proportion

4. 2:1; 4:1

5. yes

Extend

6. corresponding sides are in a ratio of 2:1; corresponding angles are congruent

7. the ratio of the areas is 4:1

8. Check student's work.

Investigate Further

9. $ILMJ \sim KOPN; KIJN \sim OLMP$

10. Answers may vary. Sample: $IL : KO$ (for $ILMJ \sim KOPN$); $KI : OL$ (for $KIJN \sim OLMP$)

11. Check students' work.

Answers (continued)

Volume   Activity 51

Investigate

1. $12 - 4x$
2. $V(x) = x \cdot x \cdot (12 - 4x) = 12x^2 - 4x^3$
3. 2
4. 16
5. $S(x) = 2 \cdot x \cdot x + 4 \cdot x \cdot (12 - 4x) = -14x^2 + 48x$
6. 1.714
7. no
8. $(2.606, 30)$; maximum volume 10.695

Extend

9. $V(x) = \pi x^2(12 - 2\pi x)$ where x is the radius of the container
10. $r = 1.273$ and $h = 4; 20.372$
11. $S(x) = 2\pi x^2 + 2\pi x(12 - 2\pi x)$
12. $r = 1.136$ and $h = 4.864$
13. The shape of a package, in addition to its weight, is an important consideration—Can the package be stacked on other packages? Can it fit into certain spaces on a truck or plane? Is it difficult to carry? etc. . . .

Rotations   Activity 52

Investigate

1. each angle $= 120$; hexagon
2. each angle 90; square
3. 100 is not a factor of 360
4. Any number that is a factor of 360 can used with a whole number amount of rotations to produce a regular polygon.

Extend

5. It is supplementary.
6. Yes
7. The angles that have a vertex at A are equal to the size of rotation. Any other pair of angles formed will be supplementary to the angle of rotation.
8. A square can be used to form a tessellation.
9. Their angles must be factors of 360.
10. The sum of the angles around any point equals 360.
11. Regular pentagons and rhombuses can be used to form a semi-pure tessellation.

Web–Based Activities   Algebra 1

Using the Web to Study Mathematics

Check students' work.

Mining Data Found on the Internet

Check students' work.

Step 1:   Winning Times for the Olympics Women's 4 × 100–meter Relay

year	52	56	60	64	68	72	76	80	84	88	92
Time	45.9	44.5	44.5	43.6	42.8	42.81	42.55	41.6	41.65	41.98	42.11

Step 2 and 3: There is a moderate linear relationship.

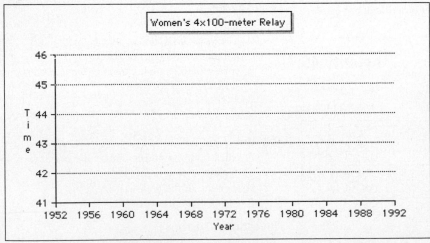

Line of best fit: $y = -0.0950681818x + 230.5653636$

Step 4: Actual 1996 Winning time: 41.95; Line of best fit prediction $= 40.80927273$; The data appears to be leveling off from 1980–1992. This would seem reasonable since winning times cannot continue to decrease at the same rate.

Answers (continued)

Generating Quizzes on the Web

Check students' work.

Graphing the Solar System

Investigate

1. 9.538
2. 0.5341
3. $b = 9.523;\ \dfrac{x^2}{9.538^2} + \dfrac{y^2}{9.523^2} = 1$
4. $\dfrac{(x + 0.5341)^2}{9.538^2} + \dfrac{y^2}{9.523^2} = 1$
5.

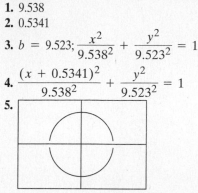

6. An eccentricity close to zero, such as 0.056, gives the appearance of a circle. Notice that the major axis, $2 \cdot 9.538 = 19.076$, is slightly larger than the minor axis, $2 \cdot 9.523 = 19.046$.

Exercises

1. The average distances to the Sun for the terrestrial planets are much closer to the Sun than the Jovian planets. A scale drawing of all nine planets would make it difficult to see the terrestrial planets.
2. Answers may vary: Pluto's average distance to the Sun is about 100 times greater than Mercury's average distance to the Sun. A sketch would need to be about 25 feet wide in order to reasonably see the orbits of all nine planets.
3. $\dfrac{x^2}{39.785^2} + \dfrac{y^2}{38.542^2} = 1$
4. Pluto's orbit is much more elliptical ($e = 0.248$) than Neptune's (which is nearly circular with $e = 0.009$). Because of this, there are times when Pluto's orbit brings the planet closer to the sun than Neptune's.
5. The earth is tilted more towards the Sun during the summer months, thereby creating a warmer climate.
6. There would be extreme temperature changes if the Earth's orbit was more elliptical.

Building a Web Page About Buildings

Check students' work.

Creating Dynamic Images for the Web

Check students' work.